ROUTLEDGE LIBRARY EDITIONS:
RENAISSANCE DRAMA

Volume 13

STUART ACADEMIC DRAMA

STUART ACADEMIC DRAMA

An Edition of Three University Plays

Edited by
DAVID L. RUSSELL

LONDON AND NEW YORK

First published in 1987 by Garland Publishing, Inc.

This edition first published in 2017
by Routledge
2 Park Square, Milton Park, Abingdon, Oxon OX14 4RN

and by Routledge
711 Third Avenue, New York, NY 10017

Routledge is an imprint of the Taylor & Francis Group, an informa business

British Library Cataloguing in Publication Data
A catalogue record for this book is available from the British Library

ISBN: 978-1-138-71372-7 (Set)
ISBN: 978-1-315-19807-1 (Set) (ebk)
ISBN: 978-1-138-23988-3 (Volume 13) (hbk)
ISBN: 978-1-138-23995-1 (Volume 13) (pbk)
ISBN: 978-1-315-29461-2 (Volume 13) (ebk)

Publisher's Note
The publisher has gone to great lengths to ensure the quality of this reprint but points out that some imperfections in the original copies may be apparent.

Disclaimer
The publisher has made every effort to trace copyright holders and would welcome correspondence from those they have been unable to trace.

Stuart Academic Drama
An Edition of
Three University Plays

edited by
David L. Russell

GARLAND PUBLISHING, INC.
NEW YORK & LONDON
1987

Library of Congress Cataloging-in-Publication Data

Stuart academic drama.

(The Renaissance imagination; v. 34)
Bibliography: p.
1. College and school drama, English. 2. English drama—17th century. I. Russell, David L., 1946– . II. Series.
PR1259.C57S78 1987 822'.3'08 87-7451
ISBN 0-8240-8414-4

Printed on acid-free, 250-year-life paper
Manufactured in the United States of America

STUART ACADEMIC DRAMA: AN EDITION OF THREE UNIVERSITY PLAYS

transcribed and edited
by

DAVID L. RUSSELL

TABLE OF CONTENTS

INTRODUCTION

The texts of the three Stuart plays in this edition have not before been transcribed and published, but have remained in an obscure commonplace book for over three centuries. While we can gather very few facts about these plays, we can with some assurance ascribe them to one of the English universities and each is indicative of a distinctly different influence on the Renaissance academic drama. _Heteroclitanomalonomia_ is part of a minor, but interesting, subgenre we can call the academic grammar play. It demonstrates the predominance of language or rhetoric studies in the period and its very subject is of purely academic interest. _Gigantomachia_ displays the continuing interest of the Renaissance in classical mythology. And _A Christmas Messe_ follows a more homely tradition, a farcical personification of the mundane. Yet all three contain a similar plot structure--a struggle between two equally strong forces, both partly right and partly wrong in their claims, and, except in the case of _Gigantomachia_, a resolution coming from a non-partisan arbiter. (_Gigantomachia_'s "arbiter" is Jove's thunderbolt--brute force, and hardly unbiased.) All three are allegorical to varying extents, albeit their messages rarely exceed the frivolous. Two contain jibes against the freshmen and various other topical allusions which substantiate their university origin. _Gigantomachia_'s origin is much less certain, and, except for some similarities to other academic dramas in its approach, and some minor pedagogical references, there is nothing concrete on which to establish it as a college play. But outside of the universities, only the Inns of Court can lay any real claim to _Gigantomachia_, and there we are on much less solid ground. Drama at the Inns of Court was characteristically much more closely aligned to the classical lmodels, following a five-act structure, using blank verse, limiting the number of characters appearing on the stage, admitting no on-stage violence, and generally observing the unities.[1] That _Gigantomachia_ violates all these premises argues against such an origin.

The manuscripts of these plays are to be found in the Folger Shakespeare Library Ms. J.a.1., a commonplace book containing seven entertainments. In addition to the three presented here, the volume includes Ben Jonson's Christmas, His Mask; John Sansbury's Periander; a Latin work, Risus Anglicanus; and a short prose drama entitled Boot and Spur. The Jonson mask has been eliminated from the present edition because it is not of academic provenance and has been previously edited. Likewise has Periander, which forms part of a St. John's College, Oxford, production of 1607, popularly called The Christmas Prince. (That whole work has been edited by F. S. Boas for the Malone Society, although Boas used a manuscript of Periander owned by St. John's College and was unaware of the existence of the Folger copy at the time.) Alfred Harbage later compared the two manuscripts and discovered the Folger to be slightly less complete (abbreviated by 60 lines, although containing three lines not in the St. John's manuscript).[2] There seems little advantage to editing an inferior copy of an already edited play of such minor significance. Since this edition has been limited to English language works, Risus Anglicanus has been omitted. But the decision to omit Boot and Spur is perhaps more arbitrary and requires more detailed explanation. This short entertainment follows the allegorical pattern of the three included here, complete with representational characters (Boots, Spurre, and so on). It is equally frivolous, consisting primarily of puns and lacking consequential action. Gerald Bentley wisely refuses a commitment, and delines to speculate further than admitting the possibility that it is a college play. Bentley notes its relationship to another known Cambridge work and assigns the work tenuously to Cambridge on the basis that "other items in the commonplace book are."[3] In the entire commonplace book, only Periander has been established as unquestionably a college play--and it belongs to Oxford. The Jonson mask is, of course, not from the universities, and the remaining five are of undetermined origin, although see the introduction to A Christmas Messe, below, for a discussion of the possible assignment to Oxford. The works to which dates can be assigned (Periander, 1607; Christmas, His Mask, 1616; and A Christmas Messe, 1619) are distributed over a dozen years, which precludes dating as a possible link, except that we can probably safely refer to all of them as "Jacobean." The point of all this is that it is impossible to infer anything about these varied pieces aside from the fact that they are bound in a single volume. The binding occurred long after their composition, and surely accident more than logic brought them together under one cover. Since our province is English academic drama, and since Boot and Spur contains neither any academic reference nor suggests the interests of the still largely classical education provided by the universities, it has been eliminated from this edition. As a prose allegorical drama about footwear without any hint of a reference to university life, it is somewhat far removed from the poetic drama and classical overtones demonstrated by the three pieces included here.

---

[1] A. Wigfall Green, The Inns of Court and Early English Drama (New York: Benjamin Blom, 1965), p. 19.

[2] "Elizabethan and Seventeenth-Century Play Manuscripts," PMLA, 50 (1935), 687-99.

[3] The Jacobean and Caroline Stage (1941-56; rpt. Oxford: Clarendon, 1949-68), V, 1345.

PART 1: COMMENTARY

I. A SURVEY OF UNIVERSITY DRAMA, 1603-1642

One published book and one unpublished dissertation constitute the principal works on English Renaissance university drama. The first is F. S. Boas' University Drama in the Tudor Age, a long-admired study; the second is Carl Stratman's "Dramatic Performances at Oxford and Cambridge, 1603-1642," intended to pick up where Boas left off. There are a handful of articles scattered about scholarly journals, G. C. Moore Smith being among the more prominent contributors. Lip service is paid by others in assorted historical surveys, but the field has been largely neglected--and particularly in recent years. Those mentioned above all date from the first half of the twentieth century.

There is, perhaps, an all-too-obvious explanation for this apparent oversight. The quality of the university drama is unquestionably second-rate (even this, in some cases, is inordinate praise). The themes are didactic, the plots imitative, the verse doggerel--by and large, the university drama was amateurish and uninnovative. Marlowe may have done some inspired writing while at Cambridge, and Lyly was strongly influenced by the college drama, but the English universities were hardly the fountainheads of the nation's literary achievement--and certainly not of its dramatic achievement. But, after all, the universities did not exactly encourage the drama, and, on occasion, did prohibit certain forms of it (more will be said of this below). The value of plays, as far as the universities were concerned, was chiefly didactic--whether they be religious and moral (as they were especially in early Tudor times) or pedagogical, introducing students to the venerated classical works and aiding their instruction in rhetoric and declamation. All this served to inhibit academic dramatic development, for the limitations would certainly discourage any dramatist of talent and originality. Even when the recreative purpose of drama gained favor in academe--at least by the turn of the seventeenth century--the college authorities must still have rigidly restricted the scholar-dramatists, for the English Renaissance universities were seldom accused of fanning flames of intellectual stimulation. However, if much of the blame for the poor quality of the academic drama must be placed on conservative university authorities, it must not be forgotten that if the London city fathers had had their way, there would have been no drama in England at all.

Tucker Brooke has referred to the universities and the Inns of Court as "the cradles of modern English drama."[1] We cannot forget Gammer Gurton's Needle, appearing at Cambridge sometime before the middle of the sixteenth century, which has been (accurately) extolled as "the most remarkable college play that has come down to us."[2] Tucker Brooke praises the university Latin plays for having "form, dignity, and intellectual wit at a time when the vernacular plays piteously lacked these things."[3] But these are estimations of the mid-sixteenth-century academic drama; the later Jacobean university drama suffers in comparison with the brilliant London stage of the period. There is always the sense, when one is examining these later academic plays, that the Pierian Spring had gone dry. There certainly are few forgotten masterpieces here.

The drama persisted at the universities, for better or for worse, throughout the Renaissance up until the Civil War. Various college records show that money was expended on dramatic productions fairly regularly through the sixteenth and first half of the seventeenth centuries.[4] But the universities appear to have been extremely parochial in their encouragement of the drama, and generally abhorred (at least officially) popular and professional drama. At Oxford, the frequenting of non-academic plays was forbidden of university students--a master, bachelor or scholar of 18 or more caught attending a public performance was imprisoned; an undergraduate under 18 suffered "open punishment" in St. Mary's Church.[5] In 1604, a royal letter forbade "unprofitable or idle games and plays" to be carried on "within five mile compass of and from the university and town" of Cambridge, especially bull-baiting, bear-baiting, common plays, publick shews, interludes, comedies and tragedies in the English tongue."[6] This latter was probably a reaction to the satires attacking the townspeople--the town/gown strife was notoriously bitter. F. S. Boas refers to the "traditional hostility to professional actors" expressed by Oxford. There are even records of the university officials paying professional troupes to vacate the college premises without performing. This happened on at least five different occasions during the reign of James I.[7] Academic snobbery may have been the reason, but the fact remains that the universities did not see fit to discontinue their own sometimes riotous productions. And, there is no question that college performances before visiting royalty and other dignitaries were sources of great pride for the universities. Despite what may have been the prevailing attitude toward the "public" theater, attendance at college performances was apparently quite acceptable at both universities. At any rate, it would have been very fatuous indeed for either university to imagine it could eradicate the dramatic entertainments which so delighted every class of Tudor and Stuart England.

Early Tudor university drama seems to have been purely recreative, but it soon was adopted for educational purposes. Boas points out that late Elizabethan academic drama served two pedagogical purposes:

> It was a handmaid both to scholarship and to rhetoric. It helped to familiarize the younger students with texts of the classical dramatists, with the practice of original composition in Latin verses or prose, even as in Bellum Grammaticale, with the elements of Latin accidence. At the same time it trained them in the art of declamation, in the management of voice and "action" . . . .[8]

But Stuart times saw once again the recreative purpose of drama flourishing in the universities, and English gradually gaining acceptance as a language of plays. (Queen Elizabeth may have found relaxation in translating Latin, but it is doubtful that many English university students chose to spend their leisure hours in linguistic pursuits.) Boas lists over one hundred university plays as belonging to the Tudor period, only twenty of which are identified as written English, the overwhelming majority being in Latin.[9] We sometimes forget how very close to the medieval world the Renaissance actually was; this university preference is solid evidence of the tenacity of medieval ideas. When the vernacular was used, it was almost exclusively for comedy. Only Latin or Greek (the latter very infrequently, since Greek studies were in a notorious state of neglect in the English Renaissance universities) were considered suitable for the graver matter of tragedy. That the vernacular was rapidly increasing in popularity among college dramatists in Jacobean times is demonstrated by Stratman's examination of Stuart academic drama. He discovered twenty-seven plays written in English out of a total of sixty-one. The wider use of English for college plays seems to reflect both the changing nature of academic drama (that is, from pedagogical to recreative) and the influence of the events occurring in the contemporary London stage, which did much to bring the English tongue into its own as a respectable means of discourse.

The records indicate that the university drama was far more seasonal than that in London (which seems to have closed up only for the plague). Students were in residence at the universities year-round, most spending their holidays in their colleges or halls. Given the rapid development of the drama during the Renaissance, it is only natural that students would turn to this form of recreation to pass their leisure time. But since a theatrical production requires considerable planning and organization, it is not surprising that the holidays (especially Christmas) saw the greatest number of performances. (We assume that during the academic term both students and teachers would be too preoccupied with scholarly pursuits to produce plays, and drama was not a normal part of the curriculum.) Two of the three plays in this edition contain direct references to their purposes as Christmas entertainments, in fact. The notable exceptions to these seasonal productions were, of course, the lavish performances for royal visitors--during which times the whole university seems to have ground to a halt in order to entertain the royal personages in the manner to which they were accustomed.

Since, as a rule, the Christmas holidays were the prime times for the academic drama, indoor productions were usual. In this respect, the university performances were more similar to the Court performances than to the open-air productions of the London theaters. By this we can assume the stages were temporary structures--if structures at all. A simple raised platform would serve for most productions. *Gigantomachia* is distinctive in calling for an upper stage, and that fact alone casts doubt on its university provenance. But an open gallery above could readily be converted to such purposes. Various college account books bear frequent reference to expenditures for lighting the halls, suggesting that the plays were generally evening performances.[10] (During the visits of both Elizabeth and James to the universities, the plays before the sovereign were always given at night--sometimes starting as late as 9:00 p.m. and lasting beyond midnight.) Costuming was often very lavish, and properties were important, if we can judge from the expenditures noted in the accounts. Once again, *Gigantomachia* is called to mind. Among the properties required would seem to be mountains! although we must suspect that players were costumed to represent these landmarks--

particularly since the mountains are listed with the Dramatis Personae. But as on all Renaissance English stages, scenery was the responsibility primarily of the audience's imagination.

These same account books also record, with alarming frequency, expenditures for replacing glass broken during performances. We know that Elizabethan and Jacobean audiences were anything but passive observers; however, the students may have had other reasons for their over-exuberant reactions to the plays. There is an immediacy about many university plays that can only be achieved when the audience and the playwright are personally acquainted, have the same daily experiences, share the same residence, eat the same food, pursue the same studies, and so on. The academic comedies and satires provide this immediacy. It is much easier to incite some innocent rowdiness in an audience which comprises friends and acquaintances than in one consisting of the general public. Heteroclitanomalonomia contains an example of this immediacy when the Chorus, at the end of the first act, pokes fun at an unnamed member of the crowd, but it is difficult to imagine this play inciting a riot. The best clue that the festival riots were harmless (outside of a few broken windows) is the fact that, while some colleges took the precaution of protecting the windows with grates, none cancelled the plays altogether.

The pomp, panoply, and enthusiasm of the university drama, Stratman attributes to the visits by King James and his family to Oxford and Cambridge. He sees these visits as the principal motivators of the academic productions. In actuality, these visits were infrequent (though, they surpassed in number those of Elizabeth, who in forty-five years on the throne saw Oxford twice and Cambridge once!). But the dramatic entertainments seem to have been the high points of the visits, and the enthusiasm which swelled for the royal performances quite likely lingered for a long time afterward, giving the university playwrights sufficient adrenaline to carry them several seasons. On the other hand, Stratman may have exaggerated the importance of these visits, and certainly, even without royal patronage, ambitious young students would have delighted in both the writing and production of plays. The theatre, after all, had become one of the most popular of all English pastimes, and, at any rate, academic drama remained apparently healthy during Elizabeth's reign, with comparatively little royal influence at the universities. Nevertheless, the royal visits of King James to the universities are prominent in dramatic history because those occasions were the only ones thought worthy of recording. The great majority of the plays we can identify as being of university origin possess nothing to suggest they were intended to curry royal favor--and that seems certainly true of the three plays in the present edition.

One important influence, however, was that of classical drama--both Greek and Latin. Plays by Sophocles, Euripides, Aristophanes, Plautus and Seneca are all recorded as having been presented at the universities as early as the mid-sixteenth century. The Greek plays, as might be expected, are somewhat less prominent, and their presentations may have been in Latin translation (this was certainly the case with Sophocles' Ajax Flagellifer, which was prepared for Queen Elizabeth at Cambridge in 1564). It was the primacy of Latin, coupled with the academic reverence for the ancients, which gave the classical playwrights inevitable significance in the universities. Performances of Plautus and Seneca can especially be noted in the Tudor period, with Plautus being extremely popular. Seneca was, of course, much admired by the Renaissance for his moral tone and sententiousness. By Stuart times such revivals of the classics seem to have declined--perhaps because there were now so many more original plays by university contemporaries available. But their influence persisted and Seneca, particularly, remained the chief model for academic tragedy throughout the period. While Plautus seems to have enjoyed the most revivals in the Tudor age and his plays afforded many dramatists with plots, a more widespread influence on academic comedy appears to have been the writers of Renaissance Italy, which, Stratman found, supplied the sources for most Stuart university plays.[11] This classical influence is of interest to us here not because the Greek and Roman dramatists were the models for any of these plays, but because the plots of at least two are strongly dependent upon classical learning. Heteroclitanomalonomia, a play about Latin grammar, could only have been written in an age which still revered the language of ancient Rome. And Gigantomachia takes as its subject a mythological story dating back at least as far as Hesiod. It is necessary to point out, however, that the classical influence in the academic drama was most prevalent in the tragedies. In their comedies, they often preferred more contemporary satire, even when it bordered on farce, for it provided better opportunity for witty display. A Christmas Messe falls into this class, for it is both very contemporary and very farcical. But in all university plays, including the three in this edition, the tone preserved was that of the medieval moralities and allegories, often heavily imbued with a didacticism which successfully averted any attempt at artistic subtlety.

Conservativism is the overwhelming characteristic of academic drama, and in the early Stuart years college dramatists became increasingly enamored of allegorical plays.[12] Schelling asserts that "it was satire and allegory which continued most to animate the drama of the colleges."[13] Especially prominent are veiled attacks on Puritanism, and the Stuart university drama began more and more to reflect the growing social unrest of the realm, with the drama, not surprisingly, aligned with the Royalist faction. The satirical and allegorical plays were derived from the medieval forms, though their subject matter was often very contemporary, sometimes dangerously political. But the medieval influence was so pervasive in college drama that it cannot be explained by politics alone. The three plays which concern us here all represent, to varying degrees, the survival of medieval allegory and satire--none, with the possible exception of *Gigantomachia* in a very peculiar way, is politically motivated to any great degree. The universities merely clung to these older forms more tenaciously than the popular stage not because satire and allegory served useful social purposes, but because these forms could be more soundly defended on the grounds of tradition and pedagogical principles. In other words, like the classical models, satire and allegory were not only entertaining, but instructive.

These, then, are the principal influences of the university drama. Of course, many plays reflect a combination of these elements. To this point, we have been considering the drama of both universities as if it were a joint venture. Naturally, this was not so. Surviving records indicate that Cambridge was far more active in the drama than Oxford. Compilations reveal three times as many productions at Cambridge as at Oxford.[14] Though there are a variety of possibilities, any explanation for these statistics would be purely speculative. Are the Oxford records less complete? Did the Oxford recorders simply fail to mention the bulk of college productions? Or did Oxford, in fact, produce fewer plays? There is another distinction that must be considered before we leave this matter. Both Boas and Stratman discovered a preponderance of comedy being produced at Cambridge, while Oxford seemed to prefer tragedy.[15] Room must, naturally, be admitted for lost plays, some Cambridge tragedies and some Oxford comedies, but it is unlikely that the predominant surviving genre in each university is purely accidental. Boas points out that the drama was much more wide-spread at Cambridge--that is, many more colleges participated than at Oxford. He further maintains that Oxford productions seem to have been much more elaborate than Cambridge ones, and that, on the whole, tragedies were more costly to produce than comedies.[16] Thus it is quite likely that the apparent favored genre at each university may only reflect financial considerations which also determined total numbers of productions.

And so we have it--plays written by students and occasionally teachers to entertain their fellows spending the holidays at college. They are encumbered with esoterica and shackled by tradition. But their usefulness as primary sources of social history has been largely overlooked. Here we learn what these people laughed at and what they sneered at. Here we learn of their daily habits and routines. True, much of this we can cull from the popular drama of London, and on a broader scale. But we must not forget that, except for the lawyers, every university-educated person in England was a product of either Oxford or Cambridge. The importance of these institutions cannot be ignored. And the entertainments their students produced and, presumably, enjoyed must be recognized as significant products of the English Renaissance social milieu. The university drama is a gap that literary historians would do well to explore. If the sources themselves are not quite neglected literary gems, they are fresh, untrammeled works with their own peculiar interest and charm and their own special reward.

---

[1] C. F. Tucker Brooke, "Latin Drama in Renaissance England," ELH, 13 (1946), 234.

[2] F. P. Wilson, The English Drama: 1485-1585, ed. G. K. Hunter (New York: Oxford University Press, 1960), p. 110.

[3] C. F. Tucker Brooke, "Latin Drama," 235.

[4] Sandra Billington cites recently discovered records of St. John's College, Cambridge, which support this position. Formerly there had been no concrete evidence of dramatic performances at St. John's between 1536 and 1555 (although other Cambridge colleges were known to have had performances during this time). The discovery of St. John's records adds that college to the list of those continually active in the drama and encourages the continued search for information on the neglected university drama. See Billington, "Sixteenth-Century Drama in St. John's College, Cambridge," Review of English Studies, 29 (1978), 1-10.

[5] Muriel St. Clare Byrne, Elizabethan Life in Town and Country (London: Methuen, 1961), pp. 134-35.

[6]Carl J. Stratman, "Dramatic Performances at oxford and Cambridge, 1603-1642," Diss. University of Illinois, Urbana, pp. 26-27.

[7]F. S. Boas, "Theatrical Companies at Oxford in the Seventeenth Century," *Fortnightly Review*, 110 (1918), 259.

[8]F. S. Boas, *University Drama in the Tudor Age* (1941; rpt. New York: Benjamin Blom, 1966), pp. 349-50.

[9]F. S. Boas, *University Drama*, pp. 386-90.

[10]Stratman, p. 38.

[11]Stratman, p. 271.

[12]F. S. Boas, "University Plays," in *The Drama to 1642: Part Two*, Vol. VI of *The Cambridge History of English Literature*, ed. A. W. Ward and A. R. Waller (Cambridge: University Press, 1961), p. 323.

[13]Felix E. Schelling, *Elizabethan Drama, 1558-1642*, II (Boston: Houghton-Mifflin, 1908), 81.

[14]See Frederick Gard Fleay, *A Chronicle History of the London Stage, 1559-1642* (London: Reeves and Turner, 1890) pp. 419-21, and Boas, *University Drama*, pp. 386-90. Boas treats only the Tudor drama, but his list is far more complete than Fleay's.

[15]Boas, *University Drama*, pp. 346-47, and Stratman, p. 268.

[16]Boas, *University Drama*, pp. 348-49.

II. THE ALLEGORICAL/DEBATE PLAY

When we are considering the influences upon the plays here edited, two elements, both medieval in their immediate origins, come to mind. The stronger influence is the allegory, which enjoyed a resurgence in popularity on the university stage during the Jacobean and Caroline periods. In actual fact, the allegory never truly fell out of favor in Tudor and Stuart England, though the relative proportion of allegorical plays did seem to increase at the universities during the reign of James I. Boas tells us that in the early Stuart years allegorical plays grew immensely in popularity among college dramatists.[1] It may be that the Oxford play, _Bellum Grammaticale_, which is significant for our present consideration, established the academic taste for allegory. This play seems to have enjoyed a considerable measure of popularity and influence, and we will be looking more closely at this piece when we examine the academic grammar plays.

The second influence, equally medieval, is the debate (or _débat_). Its origins lie in the medieval penchant for the dialogue in examining moral and philosophical issues. The most common medieval debate was that between the Body and the Soul, though familiar variations included debates between the Head and the Heart, Good Angels and Evil (in the manner of _Doctor Faustus_), and so on. The influence of the debate in the university drama is seen particularly in the rather long-winded speeches pro and con (just as one might expect from a debate exercise) and in the moralizing (which few Renaissance writers could resist).

So it is the use of allegorical characters and plots combined with the structure and technique of the debate which helped to form much of the university drama--including the three plays in this edition. For the sake of convenience we may term the plays belonging to this academic theatrical tradition "allegorical/debate" plays--with a somewhat stronger emphasis on "allegorical."

Oxford, as we have seen, has far less extant evidence of dramatic activity than Cambridge, but among the better known Oxford allegories is Barton Holyday's _Technogamia; or, The Marriages of the Arts_. This play shows how the arts and sciences attempt unnatural unions and it emerges as a quasi-philosophical treatise. Technogamia has received more attention than most academic plays, partly because its author was a friend of and admired by Anthony à Wood--an association which resulted in the benefit of Holyday's inclusion in the Athenae Oxoniensis. There are records of two performances--one before King James I at Woodstock on August 26, 1621 (though from the earlier reports of the Oxford production on February 23, 1617/18, one wonders why). Wood tells us that the first performance met "with no great applause," and the Woodstock performance seems to have been more disastrous.[2] Bentley, after a lengthy treatment of the author and the play's history, dismisses it as "simply another long-winded allegorical discussion of the curriculum and of education."[3]

A second Oxford allegorical play worth noting is Richard Zouche's The Sophister (which has a manuscript title of Fallacy; or, The Troubles of Great Hermenia). The ascription is not undisputed, and it can only be dated in a very general way between 1610 and 1631, but its university provenance is certain. The play shows Fallacy attempting to dispose of his father, Discourse, by giving him a potion. But Fallacy is challenged in his grasp for power by his brothers, Demonstration and Topicus. A fraternal dispute ensues, but all is for naught as the physician, Analysis, intervenes by curing Discourse and the defeated Fallacy flees. The author, if Zouche is indeed the author, remained in university life and achieved many academic honors, including a Regius Professorship--university drama was not necessarily the domain of carefree bohemian students with suspect scholarly pretensions.

Among the most famous of all the Oxford productions, however, is the allegorical play The Floating Island (also called Passions Calmed and Prudentius) presented at Christ Church Oxford before King Charles I and Queen Henrietta Maria on August 29, 1636. The play, by William Strode, met the good fortune of all college plays presented during Royal visits: it has been dubiously immortalized in the numerous accounts of the great occasion when the monarch condescended to be entertained by the university. Anthony à Wood provides a surprisingly detailed description of the staging, from which we learn much more about university productions than anyone ever bothered to tell us about the London playhouses. Henry Lawes, no mean composer, wrote the music for the play, and the staging was extravagant. The play depicts the passions in a state of revolt, while their king, Prudentius, retires, allowing his rebellious subjects to "hang themselves." The allegory is far more specific and political than is typical of a college drama, although it should be noted that university plays became increasingly bold in their attacks on Puritanism as the social and political climate of the realm grew more heated. That the Puritans found themselves frequent targets in the medium they so despised on principle served only to cement their disdain for the stage. Easily recognizable are the Puritan William Prynne as the antagonist, Malevolo, and the wise Prudentius is, of course, King Charles I. Such bitter anti-Puritan gibes did more than their share to hurry events along the road to the crucial year, 1642. If, as is maintained above, one of the chief importances of the academic plays is historical, The Floating Island has manifold significance for the student of early seventeenth-century political and well as social history. Its neglect is not entirely deserved.

As might be expected, Cambridge provides us with many more allegorical plays than Oxford. We will consider only a few of the better-known, yet still characteristic, ones. Among the earliest of the Jacobean efforts is Thomas Tomkis' Lingua; or, The Combat of the Tongue and the Five Senses for Superiority, published in 1607, though dating from possibly 1602/03.[4] In this play, Lingua, the tongue, attempts to vindicate her claim to be a sixth sense. The principal characters, beside Lingua, include the Five Senses (Auditus, Tactus, Visus, Olfactus, and Gustus) and two old men, Communis Senses (Common Sense) and Memoria. The Five Senses refuse Lingua's claim, and she sets about, with the aid of Mendacio (Liar), to breed strife among the Senses in the hope of reaping reward from the resulting contention. She uses a device similar to the goddess Eris when she tossed the legendary golden apple onto the Olympian banqueting table and provoked the series of events leading to the fall of Troy. Instead of a golden apple, Lingua leaves in the Senses' path a crown and robe inscribed with:

> Hee of the fiue that proves himselfe the best
> Shall haue his Temples with this Coronet blest.

The quarrel among the Senses does arise and Communis Senses staves off a disastrous fight by ordering the five to appear before his Court and present their special qualities for him to judge. Their various presentations go on at great length, and at last, for reasons that are difficult to comprehend,

Visus ("the author in inuention") is offered the crown, and the robe is given to Auditus, because he augments invention. Communis Senses also dismisses Lingua's claim:

> wherefore wee iudge you to be no Sense simply, onely thus much we from hence forth pronounce, that all women for your sake shall have six Senses, that is seeing, hearing, tasting, smelling, touching, and the last and feminine sense, the sense of speaking.

Enraged, Lingua attempts one more time to instigate a quarrel, but this time is found out, committed to Gustus' custody and he is to

> keepe her vnder the custody of two strong doores, euery day till she come to 80 years of age, see she be well guarded with 30 tall watchmen, without whose license shee shall by no means wagge abroad, neuertheless vse her Lady-like according to her estate.

Lingua was extraordinarily popular and is superior in quality to most university plays. The play was even honored with a tradition that Oliver Cromwell acted in it as a boy.

Pathomachia; or, The Battell of Affections has been from time to time attributed to Tomkis, also. However, the play was published in 1630 in an edition which refers to the "deceased author." Since Tomkis died no earlier than 1634, the epithet would have been premature and therefore argues against Tomkis' authorship. The play closely resembles Lingua, and G. C. Moore Smith sees the two as complementary, though Pathomachia seems to have been written about 1615, several years after Lingua. That it is actually a university play is only speculation, and Bentley's remark, "Probably no other Jacobean audience would have listened to such an involved allegorical presentation of psychology," tells us as much about university drama in general as it does about Pathomachia. The allegory treats the revolt of the Affections against Love and Hatred--thus following the same general pattern of other allegories we have considered, but with a difference. The medium is prose, unusual in a college play, though apparently much more common for these tragi-comic allegories than for other types, for the next two plays to be considered are also prose.

About the same time to which Pathomachia is assigned, Cambridge saw the production of several other allegorical plays. Exchange Ware, perhaps better known as Band, Cuffe, and Ruffe, saw two editions in 1615.[5] Following a new familiar pattern, the play concerns a quarrel between Band and Ruffe, with Cuffe drawn in as arbiter. It is not without humor, chiefly arising from puns about clothing. In the heat of the argument, Band cries:

> Nay, braggart, is not your great words can carrie it away so; giue Band but a hemme, and hee will be for you at any time, name the place, the time and houre of our meeting.

Ruffe replies:

> The place, the Paper-Mills, where I will teare thee into Rags, before I have done with thee: the time, tomorrow in the after-noone about one: but you heare: wee will single, you shall be double, Band.

To himself, Cuffe mutters:

> Now I perceiue, the Spaniard and the Hollander will to it roundly.

Of course, no agreement can be reached, and Cuffe is called upon to bring this resolution:

> Well then, thus I pronounce. Ruffe shall be most accounted of amongst the Clergie, for he is the grauer Fellow. (Although I know, the Puritans will not greatly care for him hee hath such a deale of settin, and they love standing better.) As for you, Band, you shall bee most made of amongst the young Gallants (although sometimes they shall vse Ruffe, for a fashion, but not otherwise;) how euer, you neede not regard the giddie headed miltitude, let them doe as they list, sometimes respecting one, sometimes the other; but when you come to the Counssilors, and men of Law, which know right from wrong, acknowledging both Worths to be equall, they shall perferre neither, but vse the kindnesse of you both, wearing both a Band and a Ruffe.[6]

Similar to Band, Cuffe, and Ruffe, both in its punning and resolution, is Worke for Cutlers; or, a Merry Dialogue Betweene Sword, Rapier, and Dagger. It also dates from about 1615 at Cambridge. This time, Dagger takes the place of Cuffe, saying:

> Nay Sword, put the Case of Rapiers aside, that there were two of them, I hope you were able to buckle with them.

Sword denigrates Rapier as a "base Spaniard," and Rapier in turn challenges him to a duel. Dagger threatens to

> sende one after you, which shall scoure you both. The Cutler can doe it. I have seene him handle you both brauely.

Still they are determined to fight, interrupted first by a discussion of the ancestry of Sword; but Rapier is full of scorn. Then follows a discussion of the relative merits of military weapons. Finally, Dagger persuades them to permit him to mediate, and he proceeds in a fashion typical of the arbiters in these plays:

> Then in briefe it shall bee thus. Sworde, you shall beare Chiefe force ith Campe, and be made Generall of the Field, to veare way euery where. As for you Rapier, since Duels are put downe, you shall liue quietly and peaceablie here 'ith Court,

> and goe euery day in Veluet: you shall be Frends with euerie one, and bee on euery ones side, that if occasion serue, and Sworde be absent, so that matters are driuen to a push, Rapier, shall be the onely man to performe a Cambate: And I my selfe will backe you both, as occasion shall serue.[7]

The Cambridge comedy, Fucus Histriomastix, probably by Robert Ward and dating sometime around 1622 or 1623, openly attacks Puritan hypocrisy, especially the Puritan attitude toward the theater. Fucus Histriomastix, secretly depraved and iniquitous, is indefatigable in his warfare against the university drama. This battle, we are told, is only the most recent in a long line of self-righteous contests against "popular ballads, bagpipes, dancing, wine bibbing, saints' days and maypoles."[8] Fucus arrives in Cambridge during the preparations for the marriage between Iudicium's son, Philomathes, and Comoedia, the daughter of Ingenitum and Poetice. Fucus works on Iudicium, inducing him to call off the wedding. At this point the customary debate presenting the arguments for and against the academic drama occurs. After considerable intrigue, Fucus is discovered for the scoundrel he is and suffers ridicule from all his enemies. Of course, the marriage takes place. The play has a subplot--the love affair of Villenus, a countryman, and Ballada, who is Ingenitum's illegitimate daughter by Phantasia. Fucus is equally unsuccessful in his attempts to foil that union. As can be seen, the basic elements of the allegorical/debate play are there, though the structure is more complicated than most amateurish efforts which would not be bothered with the interweaving of a parallel underplot.

The pattern of the allegorical/debate play must by now be familiar. The characters, who are representational, are thrown into a conflict of ideas. The opposing sides are given their opportunities to present their cases (if not to each other at least to the audience) and the resolution generally comes from a third, disinterested party. Both Heteroclitanomalonomia and A Christmas Messe follow the pattern religiously. Gigantomachia does not fit in so tidily as we might like, unless we accept the hypothesis presented in Section VI below that the play is a political allegory, if a rather frivolous and heavily-disguised one.

The persistence of the allegorical/debate play as a popular academic form helps to account for the retarded development of university drama. Stratman's contention that the Royal visits of the Stuarts to the universities provided the principal stimulus for college drama may, in part, be substantiated. But that influence, we must remember, did no great service to the popular drama either. The courts of both James I and Charles I were inclined to spectacle, and if James seemed to prefer more substance than his son, it was a pedantic preference for moralizing and certainly not one for provocative drama. Allegorical plays provided spectacle with their richly-attired, sometimes fantastic, personifications, and the debate element provided opportunities for declamation but hardly for real dramatic conflict. Rather than seeing the Royal patronage of the universities as influencing the course of academic drama, we might be more accurate in seeing the Royal tastes as consonant with the type of play the universities had long been accustomed to producing and which had persisted long enough to finally find an appreciative Royal audience.

---

[1] Frederick S. Boas, University Drama in the Tudor Age (1914; rpt. New York: Benjamin Blom, 1966), p. 323.

[2] See Gerald Bentley, The Jacobean and Caroline Stage (1941-56; rpt. Oxford: Clarendon, 1948-68), IV, 590; Anthony a Wood, Athenae Oxonienses, ed. Philip Blin (London: F. C. & J. Rivington, 1813-20), III, 522; J. B. Nichols, The Progresses, Processions, and Magnificent Festivities of King James the First, His Royal Consort, Family and Court (London: J. B. Nichols, 1828), IV, 713-15 and 1108-12; and Sister M. Jean Carmel Cavanaugh's edition of Technogamia, pp. xxix-xlii.

[3] Bentley, IV, 596.

[4] All references to this play are to Thomas Tomkis, Lingua in Robert Dodsley, A Select Collection of Old English Plays, 4th ed., W. Carew Hazlitt, ed. (1874-76; rpt. New York: Benjamin Blom, 1964).

[5] All references to this play are to Pathomachia, ed. Paul Edward Smith (Washington, D. C.: The Catholic University Press, 1942).

[6] Carl J. Stratman, "Dramatic Performances at Oxford and Cambridge, 1603-1642." Diss. University of Illinois, Urbana, 1947, pp. 168-69.

[7] Stratman, pp. 170-70b.

[8] Stratman, p. 112.

III. THE ACADEMIC GRAMMAR PLAY:

HETEROCLITANOMALONOMIA

Renaissance England has a minor, as yet largely unexplored, dramatic tradition which has been aptly termed the academic grammar play.[1] The tradition seems to have begun with the Italian Andreas Guarna's curious discourse, Bellum Grammaticale, published in Cremona, Italy, in 1511. This Latin prose work proposes to explain the irregularities of Latin grammar as resulting from a war between the two grammar kings, Poeta (Noun) and Amo (Verb). Among the other characters are Participle, Adjective, Adverb, Conjunction, all residents of the mythical Grammar-Land. The quarrel of the joint rulers led to a great battle, causing the alignment of their subjects upon one side or the other. The slaughter in the resulting conflict was so extreme that both kings were willing to submit to arbitration by three Italian humanists. A compromise, granting certain prerogatives to each king, was achieved, and thus Latin grammar and its irregularities emerged. Somewhat less than fascinating reading for us today, the work was one of the most popular in the Renaissance literary world, and went through at least seventy-five known editions in the sixteenth century alone. While Guarna's Latin found its way into editions in Italy, Spain, France, Germany, Switzerland, the Netherlands, and Denmark, it oddly enough was not published in the British Isles until 1623 at Aberdeen, Scotland.[2] But an English translation by William Hayward did appear perhaps as early as 1569, though the earliest extant copy of his work is an edition from 1576.[3]

The next noteworthy event in our chronicle occurred on Sunday, 24 September 1592, at Christ Church College, Oxford. A contemporary account reads:

> At night there was a comedy acted before hir Highnes in the hall of that Colledge; and one other on Tuesday at night, being both of them but meanly performed (as we thought), and yet most graciouslye, and with great patience, heard by hir Majestie. The one being called "Bellum Grammaticale," and the other intituled "Riuales."[4]

This is, of course, a reference to the second visit of Queen Elizabeth to Oxford University, and the report is that of Philip Stringer, who as a drama critic seems to have been notoriously difficult to please.[5]

Bellum Grammaticale was a revival and may have been written as early as 1583 by Leonard Hutten.[6] Despite or because of the fact that it was in Latin and contained rather weighty allegory, it was one of the most popular of Elizabethan university dramas. Records show that as late as 1718, Bellum Grammaticale was acted at Tonbridge School.[7]

The dramatization greatly modifies Guarna's plot--sometimes for obvious dramatic purposes. Among the principal changes are supplying the two kings with parasites (in the manner of Roman comedy); casting Poeta into melancholy (only his parasite's promptings cause him to declare war); gibing at the Papacy (Guarna's work had ended with a compliment to Julius II); giving less prominence to the battle itself (Guarna had devoted one-third of his work to it); and replacing the Italian arbiters with the Belgian grammarian Jean Despauteres (Despauterius), and the Englishmen, Linacre and William Lily.[8]

It is not surprising that so popular a work inspired imitators. Louise B. Morgan reports three appearing during the seventeenth century: Princeps Rhetoricus (1648) by John Mason of Catherine Hall, Cambridge; The Warr of Grammar, also called Basileia seu Bellum Grammaticale (acted by the Cranebrook School in 1666) often ascribed to Samuel Hoadley, and closely following, but not an exact translation of, Hutten's Latin; and Words Made Visible (1679), an anonymous work in two parts, the first of which follows closely both The Warr of Grammar and Bellum Grammaticale.[9] And, we are told, that in December 1717, at Stamford School, still another adaptation of Guarna's work, this entitled Bellum Grammaticale, siue de Bello Nominem et Verborum Fabula, was presented.[10]

The academic grammar play, naturally, would only be tolerated by an audience of very specialized tastes. The sub-genre speaks to the high regard in which grammar and rhetoric were held in Renaissance England--or more accurately, among the academicians of Renaissance England. These are not plays for the masses. But neither are they great dissertations of learning or morality, although they owe much in structure to the later medieval drama which did often profess these higher principles. Instead, they are playful pieces often stepping into the realm of absurdity, though always remaining faithful in detail to the principles of Latin grammar on which their plots are based. The university audience remained pedantic, even when having fun--rather like today's academic audiences.

It is to this tradition of academic grammar plays that Heteroclitanomalonomia belongs--a tradition which makes up in durability what it lacks in luster. There is no question that this work was influenced by Guarna, Hayward, and Hutten, or some combination of them. But its author is no slavish imitator, though, given his slight dramatic capacity, this may be regrettable. The manuscript bears the date 1613, which makes Heteroclitanomalonomia the earliest extant academic grammar play written in English that has yet come to light.

Heteroclitanomalonomia appears to owe very little to Hutten's work. Indeed, the borrowings from Hutten seem restricted to the substitution of Lily as the chief arbiter (though our anonymous author diverges from all his predecesssors in using only two arbiters--Lily and the mysterious Robinson), and the de-emphasis of the battle itself. The additions of the Pedlar of Barbaria (Absurdo) and Mr. Ignorance seem original, as is the introduction of Qyeen Oratio. It is true that the basic struggle, the rallying of the subjects behind their respective leaders, the injury to Priscian during his futile attempt as peacemaker, and the severity of the losses in battle are all key elements in Guarna. And so, too, is the romancing of Participium by both kings--and in both works that opportunist decides to remain neutral, hoping to reap benefit from the victorious side. But, it is thus only in its general outline that Heteroclitanomalonomia is indebted to its predecesssors; its own variations are too significant to pass it off as only a rewriting of an earlier work.

In its Latin allusions, in fact, the play is heavily dependent upon William Lily's Shorte Introduction of Grammar. This work, by the grandfather of Euphues' author, was the most popular and influential of all Latin grammar texts, and was still widely used the later nineteenth century when the study of Latin began to fall from fashion.[11] It was divided into two parts: A Shorte Introduction of Grammar, a Latin grammar in English, and Brevissima Institutio, a somewhat lengthier grammar written in Latin. Throughout the work are scattered Latin quotations from the classical writers, and these same quotations are the ones which turn up in Heteroclitanomalonomia. Nearly all the Latin appearing in the play consists of aphoristic expressions, drawn chiefly from the classics, and nearly all of these are quoted in Lily--a fact undoubtedly readily recognizable by the play's intended audience. Given the importance of the character of Lillie as a chief arbitrator in the play, there is little question that the author was using him as his source, rather than the Latin works themselves. One lengthier passage in English (lines 123 and following) is taken verbatim from the English part of Lily's brief glossary at the end of the Brevissima Institutio. In one instance (lines 615-16) it is arguable that the author even has Lily's format in mind in order to press a joke. Almost surely, the author is depending (as well as he could) upon the audience's intimate familiarity with Lily for much of his humor. It is primarily Mr. Ignorance who throws out the Latin expressions. The learned characters, Lillie and Robinson, and even the Kings only rarely use anything but English. The Latin used by Mr. Ignorance seems intended to underscore his own pretensions and foolishness, for he speaks in cliches, often inappropriate ones, and cliches that any Renaissance schoolboy could cull with little difficulty from his grammar text. Mr. Ignorance, in other words, plays the grammar fop. His foolishness results from his inability to recognize himself as the butt of his own gibes and his attacks on the ignorant and incompetent grammar school teachers (lilnes 615 and following) are, in effect, self-deprecating.

In addition to the plot alterations and the play's much greater dependence upon Lily, Heteroclitanomalonomia differs from its more famed predecessor, Bellum Grammaticale, in its self-professed university allegory. The epilogue, spoken by Parenthesis, attempts to explain the allegorical representations: the rebellious nouns and verbs are the freshmen rebelling "ageinst us seniors" (which would seem to verify student authorship), Absurdo and Mr. Ignorance are the "ill pperties" or foolish character traits of the freshmen, Priscian represents the necessary discipline of academic life. Quite likely, the allegory was even more particular, with real-life counterparts recognizable in certain characters. The chorus following the first act makes reference--though not by name--to a specific individual (one who was known as "neat," probably here meaning "fastidious"). It is not clear whether this person was a member of the audience or one of the players, but is obvious that both actors and observers knew who was intended. The university dramatist had the dubious advantage of knowing his audience, perhaps intimately. While this may have made it easier to write a crowd-pleaser, it encouraged an abundance of esoterica which other, more diverse, audiences find tiresome.

This brings us to another minor issue which deserves mention. Twice in the play (lines 149 and 465) there are references to going about to "all the country schooles" or asking "the next schoole leave to play." College actors were amateurs at best, and it seems unlikely that these entertainments would be intended for itinerant performances. Nor do there seem to be records of such performances. But that leaves us at a loss to explain these references. Since the subject hinges so directly upon scholastic matters and one of the play's principal sources was the official grammar text of the realm, it is not out of the question that grammar schools would have had some appreciation for the play's pedagogical value. But since we have no evidence that the play was presented even at its own college, all this must remain speculative. What we know for sure is that the allegory is about college life and the typical complaints of the upperclassmen against the freshmen.

Aside from its debt to the medieval allegorical tradition, _Heteroclitanomalonomia_ draws a great deal from the earlier Tudor moralities and interludes. Ignorance and Absurdo seem to be directly adopted from the medieval drama, for both are allegorical representations of the kind that can be found in any morality or interlude. Both characters are reminiscent of the temptation or vice figures of the earlier plays, whose mischievous meddling was always aimed at bringing the weak and vulnerable to their camp. Absurdo, the pedlar, announces that his fame has spread "through most nations, / For bringing up strange orders, & new fashions." In the interlude _Hyckescorner_, the title character, whose role is to entice Frewyll and Imaginacyon down the primrose path, brags, "I have been in many a countre," and proceeds to list his extensive travels and exploits. Absurdo is his counterpart, the vagabond tempter, collecting for sale discarded Latin usages, and his efforts can only serve to debase the language. At one point, just before his departure, he launches into a frivolous sales jingle. Ditties of this sort can be found throughout the moralities and interludes, and usually with greater frequency. Absurdo's song seems a direct descendant of this medieval tradition.

Like Absurdo, Ignorance seems directly taken from the medieval drama. As the personification of one of the most common human foibles, his presence should not be too surprising. A character of the same sort is found in Wit and Science, and his close relatives are to be seen in Folye in Mundus et Infans and Nought in Mankind. As their precursors, both Ignorance and Absurdo provide an element of comic relief, and neither becomes a serious threat. The positive influences of Lillie and Robinson happily come to the salvation of Grammar-Land and disperse the meddlesome threat.

It is Participium who holds the balance of power; he is the opportunist waiting to see where the best advantage lies before claiming his allegiance. In his first scene, in fact, there are hints of his becoming the Vice figure, interested only in his own self-aggrandizement. He relates to the audience the overtures imploring his support which he has received from the two kings, and responds, "Though I love you, beleeve me I had rather / Pleasure my selfe then both." But Participium does not fulfill his promise as a Vice. In fact, before long we find him aiding in the arraignment of the rebels and bidding Lillie and Priscian, "Good Sirs be freinds, from words growes blows at length, / Pray lett us loose noe more of Grammers strength." In the final analysis, his influence, which is still considerable, is used for the country's benefit, and we are at a loss to explain these unexpected heroics. However, we cannot ignore the fact that Participium has seemed to have accomplished his goal of reaping great benefit from the struggle. From the standpoint of consistency of characterization, however, we miss any suggestion that Participium feels his accomplishment to be a self-interested victory.

In Act 4, Scene 3, a new and fully-unexpected character is introduced--Robin Robinson. The identification of this character presents the single most tantalizing question of the play. Outside of the grammarians Lily and Priscian, he is the only character not given a grammatical, allegorical name, which leads us to suspect he is an historical personage--although without the repute of the other two. There seem to be two likely possibilities--he is either another grammarian who exercised some influence or a personal acquaintance of the author and his audience. Both possibilities encounter significant obstacles. Pollard and Redgrave list but a handful of published authors named Robinson. Only one, a Hugh Robinson, can lay any claim to being a grammarian, with his 1616 work, the three-part, Preces, Grammaticalia Quaedam, Rhetorica

Brevis. However, the work bears little relationship to a grammar and even less to the rather academic concerns of Heteroclitanomalonomia. There is no evidence from Hugh Robinson's writing that grammar was one of his particular interests.

Too, the Robinson in the play is specifically called "Robin" and this causes us to consider more carefully a second Robinson, whose Christian name happens to have been Robert (for which Robin is, of course, a nickname). Robert Robinson is known from a single, curious work, The Art of Pronuntiation, published in 1617 in London. He seems to have been a teacher, but nothing for sure is known of him. His work is not a grammar, but one of the earliest efforts to study pronunciation and sounds in order to establish some linguistic standards. His work develops a detailed phonetic transcription, long ante-dating the International Phonetic Alphabet. He experiments with his system by transcribing Barnfield's Lady Pecunia. There is much evidence against his being the play's Robinson--his work appeared not at the universities but in London; he may never have been at the universities; publication of The Art of Pronuntiation follows the writing of the play by four years, so the work itself could have had no influence; and the character's function betrays none of the specific interests of Robinson's work. The evidence in his favor includes the fact that the single surviving text of his work is in the Bodleian, and, from all evidence, appears to have always been there--in other words, a connection with the university is possible. In his twentieth-century edition of The Art of Pronuntiation, E. J. Dobson admits the possibility that the work may have been written long before it was published--Barnfield's poem appeared in 1605, and it would seem reasonable that Robinson would have selected a current piece of literature to experiment with.[12] Although the character in the play gives us nothing specific to suggest Robert Robinson, his interest in correctness and maintaining standards comes close to the latter's temperament. At any rate, the complexity of The Art of Pronuntiation, albeit brief, suggests it was several years in the creating. It may be far-fetched to speculate that Robinson was at one of the universities and that his experimental thinking was known to the playwright and his audience, but in the absence of any clear explanation of the origin of the play's Robinson, no possibilites can be ignored. At the very best, he has in common with Lily and Priscian a fervent desire for standards and a relatively new approach to language analysis. And, one other thing is certain, neither Robinson's method nor this play caught on, and both passed into obscurity. The issue remains a tantalizing enigma.

Little need to be said of the play's language. The verse is written in rhymed couplets of iambic pentameter with an all-too-frequent reliance upon triple rhyme. Much of it does not rise above doggerel, although there is an occasional striking image--for example, when the blood streaking down Priscian's wounded head is described as "the Red-worme crawling downe his pate." But this is the extent of poetic value in the work. English and Latin are rather freely used interchangeably, and to appreciate much of the punning requires a fair knowledge of Latin.

The staging is extraordinarily simple and requires hardly any properties aside from a few papers and those curious semi-hoops that the Chorus carries on to suggest parentheses. The play is highly verbal--appropriate given its plot and subject--and is devoid of any physical activity. Despite its verbosity, the play does generally maintain the audience's interest, for the language is sufficiently lively to compensate for the lack of action.

Any attempt to hold up this play as a minor triumph or an unjustly neglected work of the Jacobean university stage would be sheer nonsense. It is fair to say, however, that despite its overwhelming shortcomings, it is not dull or without its own peculiar, sometimes rewarding, interests. And, the play is an important link in that curious sub-genre--the academic grammar play.

---

[1] Louise B. Morgan, "Some Academic Grammar Plays," Modern Language Review, 5 (1910), 199.

[2] Frederick S. Boas, University Drama in the Tudor Age (1914; rpt. New York: Benjamin Blom, 1966), pp. 259-60.

[3] Boas, University Drama, p. 256 and Andreas Guarna, Bellum Grammaticale: A Discourse of Gret War and Dissention betweene Two Worthy Princes, the Noune and the Verbe, tr. W[illiam] H[ayward] (London, 1576). Hayward's translation might be more accurately called a rendition, for he takes the liberty of making substantive alterations. He includes some anti-papal remarks and omits Italian localisms characteristic of the original. It whould be noted, however, that in both an epistle attached to the work (see sig. A, fol. 5^r) and in the "Preface," Hayward writes that he had

translated from the French and not from the original Latin. The question of accuracy of translation does not concern us here; the significance of all this for our purposes is that it may suggest that no Latin version was readily available in England. Thus Hayward resorted to using a French translation. Consequently, this increases the likelihood that Hutten may have had to use Hayward's translation and not Guarna's original as his source for his dramatization to be discussed shortly. In other words, Hayward may be much more significant as an influence on the English academic grammar play than Guarna.

[4]Philip Stringer, "The Grand Reception and Entertainment of Queen Elizabeth at Oxford in 1592," in Elizabethan Oxford: Reprints of Rare Tracts, ed. Charles Plummer (Oxford: Clarendon Press, 1887), p. 255.

[5]Charles Edward Mallett, The Sixteenth and Seventeenth Centuries, Vol. II of A History of the University of Oxford (New York: Longmans, Green and Co., 1924), 153.

[6]Boas, University Drama, p. 256.

[7]Boas, University Drama, p. 266.

[8]See Boas' discussion of this play in University Drama, pp. 254-67.

[9]Morgan, "Some Academic Grammar Plays," 199-200.

[10]Boas, University Drama, p. 266.

[11]Vincent J. Flynn, "Introduction," in William Lily, A Shorte Introduction of Grammar (1567; rpt. New York: Scholars' Facsimiles & Reprints, 1945), p. x.

[12]For a detailed discussion of Robert Robinson, see the "Introduction," in Robert Robinson, Phonetic Writings, ed. E. J. Dobson, Early English Text Society, Original Series, No. 238 (New York: Oxford University Press, 1957) and for a discussion of Robinson's work, see E. J. Dobson, "Robert Robinson and His Phonetic Transcripts of Early Seventeenth-Century English Pronunciation," Transactions of the Philological Society, 1947 (London: David Nutt, 1948), pp. 25-63.

IV. ALLEGORICAL SATIRE?: *GIGANTOMACHIA*

Gigantomachia bears no date, but has generally been assigned to the same decade--1610-1619--as the two other plays in this edition. that the manuscript is found in the same commonplace book as *Heteroclitanomalonomia* and *A Christmas Messe* does not guarantee its university provenance necessarily, for the volume also contains a Jonson mask. Indeed, there is much to suggest that the play is not a college production. Of the three plays in the present edition, *Gigantomachia* alone contains no internal reference to college life. Scattered throughout the play are terms which seen to have been archaic even in the early seventeenth century. The language, at any rate, is far more difficult than that of the other two plays. Except for a single reference to Lily's *Grammar*, there is nothing in the play to suggest any scholarly interest, and Lily's *Grammar* was a work that every English schoolboy would have known well. The plot would, on the surface, seem to be academic in nature--the classical story of the giants' revolt against the Olympian gods. But no classical source is faithfully adhered to, and the basic story would have been widely familiar to any grammar school pupil. In fact, *Gigantomachia* is unusual in its lack of reliance upon classical myth.

The classical accounts of this revolt--Hesiod and Ovid wrote the two most famous--are brief and decidedly unexciting. The Titans attempted to overthrow the newly-enthroned gods, only to be quelled after a brief struggle by the wrath and might of Jupiter. Some mountains were moved around, but the whole episode was rather inconsequential. It was probably unfortunate that the playwright lacked the wisdom of his classical sources in recognizing the futility in further dramatizing the event. Great, even marginally-good drama is possible only when mortality is an issue. Immortal gods fighting inhuman giants limits the dramatic possibilities. It is not even sufficient to say that the playwright was attempting a burlesque which would thereby justify his approach. A successful mock-heroic requires clear and consistent comic undertones.

Hesiod reports the violent battle in which the monsters called from the depths by Zeus hurled "showers of three hundred stones" which "darkened the Titans with a cloud of missles."[1] Hesiod's description of the conflict resembles that in Gigantomachia, though it must be understood that any description of such a conflict would resemble any other and Hesiod was not the immediate source--only the ancestor. The Titans are replaced by "Gyants," all with absurdly-descriptive names--Bouncbigge, Rumble, Thunderthwart, Hugehigh, and so on.

The play opens with Jupiter's usurpation of Saturn's throne. The giants, taking advantage of the recent revolt, decide to plot a revolt of their own, and they are not entirely without the audience's sympathy--for they are "earths sonnes" and resent the takeover of their domain by the Olympian overlords. And, too, the example of one rebellion could only encourage another. But, of course, Renaissance thought would have little respect for such a "peasants' revolt." The giants are clearly represented as oppressed, lower class ruffians--peasant, if you will. It is, however, their peasantry which is emphasized beyond their oppression. And,the giants are deprived of any respectable arguments. Bouncbigge, indeed, in a premature division of war spoils, lays claim to Diana as his spouse. Bumbcrack is anxious to have Jove's cupbearer, Ganymede, fill the giants' cups. The giants appear to crave only lust and power, and therefore lose any sympathy they may have garnered from the audience for being the down-trodden. Furthermore, Jupiter's effort at diplomacy (he sends Mercury to offer pardons if peace is achieved) fails--the giants understand no reason, only brute force. The giants and the gods finally meet, exchange verbal insults and then fight--but the battle is pitifully brief and the giants are defeated at once when Jupiter produces his secret weapon, Thunderbolt. Bouncbigge delivers a dying speech, but no serious moral can be derived from anything. The allegory treats a familiar theme--unlawful rebellion crushed by the rightful authorities. And this might be a sufficient theme were there not serious questions as to Jupiter's rightful authority, having just effected a rebellion himself against his own father.

Lest we make too much of this seriousness of purpose, it should be pointed out that the giants seem very much butts of comedy. They speak as country bumpkins--a fact that would undoubtedly have been very apparent to a Renaissance audience. They corrupt Latin terms, and throughout the play the giants are called boors, churls and other such derisive terms for the unlettered. The giants are very thinly-disguised English rustics. But the playwright fails to develop this comic possibility. He even includes the mock-heroic counterpart of the beautiful noblewoman, the giantess Rouncivall, but typically neglects to use her to any effect--either comic or dramatic.

Despite all their blustering, the giants quickly meet defeat after their confrontation with the gods. Jupiter loses all patience and calls in his thunderbolt which acts as a _deus ex machina_ to settle all affairs. It is a _deus ex machina_ in the true, traditional sense, for the audience is entirely unprepared for it, and it swiftly ends the conflict. This scene exists in two versions, a revision having been inserted, probably by someone other than the original playwright. In the revision, the giants are all slain (the original has them only wounded except for Bouncbigge who dies in both versions). This very decisive and drastic conclusion leaves little room for light-hearted mock-heroism. The fact that this final scene has been revised would strongly suggest that the play was indeed performed--and perhaps more than once, its producers apparently seeing room for improvement.

But it is easy to dwell on the play's dramatic shortcomings. It should be recognized that there is a real attempt to distinguish between levels of language. The Olympian gods are consistently given more elevated lines, while the giants are clearly intended to represent an uneducated class. It is a distinction not attempted in either _Heteroclitanomalonomia_ or _A Christmas Messe_. This is probably intended to align the audience's sympathies with the Olympians and certainly follows the classical myth's characterization of the Titans as the barbaric, unrefined earth forces. It is only modern-day, democratic ideologues or latter-day romantics who would be captivated by the charming rusticity of the giants.

Indeed, we may be delving too far if we search for politcal allegory, but it is tempting to see the giants' rebellion as a peasants' revolt firmly put down by the rightful authority of the aristocracy. True, we cannot ignore the fact that the play opens with the Olympians imprisoning their own father, Saturn, whose power they have lately usurped. But everyone knew that Saturn was an impossible tyrant who devoured his own children. From a dramatic standpoint, the inclusion of the scene with Saturn is effective, because it helps justify the giants' belief in their right to revolt. From the standpoint of the Renaissance political philosophy, however, it might be considered a fact best overlooked. The Tudors never liked to be reminded of Bosworth Field. A throne claimed by violence, no matter how justified, was always less secure than one claimed by birthright. Of course, by the time James I was called to the English throne, those memories--and most competitors--were gone, but James was a thorough Renaissance prince in his espousal of the doctrine of divine right. It is, at any rate, quite clear which is the favored side in the play. And it is no accident that the favored side has decidedly aristocratic appearances and attitudes--this is Renaissance England.

It has been mentioned in Chapter II above that Gigantomachia only tenuously fits into the allegorical mode. If it does have allegorical implications, they are political in nature. Both universities saw a great number of political allegories emerge on their stages during the early Stuart years--The Floating Island is only the msot famous. Politics and religion were impossibly intertwined, and not surprisingly, the universities, recognizing whence their fortunes came, generally sided with the King and the High Church. The Puritans were perennially attacked for what the universities saw as hypocrisy. The King was naturally held up as the fountain of wisdom. Satire in the university drama was usually heavily-veiled to avoid clashing with the authorities, who had always viewed drama in their institutions with considerable suspicion anyway. The point of all this is that Gigantomachia may well have been allegorical and satirical, its purpose sufficiently concealed to prevent negative repercussions.

There is one element in the play which leads us to suspect that there is more there than meets the eye in terms of allegory--the intriguing card-game framework. The Knave of Clubs acts as Prologue and emerges occasionally as Chorus throughout the play. He clearly establishes the card game, Ruffe (probably because of the pun on the title and not because the specific game rules are appropriate), as a metaphor for the play's action. The apparent relationship seems so loose we begin to wonder why the playwright bothered. It is interesting to note that in 1643, a political pamphlet appeared which bore the title, "The Knave of Clubs." It was an allegory representing the "artful dodges" of cardsharpers. But close beneath the surface were easily-recognized references to current political events. Further and, for our purposes, even more interesting, the pamphlet's allegorical characters are mythological.[2] Though it is possible that as many as three decades separate the writing of the play and the publication of the pamphlet, and thought there are significant differences in approach, the parallelisms that do exist suggest that there might well be more to Gigantomachia than is apparent at a cursory glance.

A word should be said of staging. Of the three plays in this edition, this one makes the most demands of a producer. The properties include mountians to be borne on the backs of the giants. An upper stage is also requried, which is somewhat unusual for a university production, although there is no reason to believe that ingenious college could not have improvised. This is the only one of the three plays in which there is an attempt at real action on the stage--the entrance of Thunderbolt and his subsequent slaying of the giants. But action alone does not make a successful play.

Gigantomachia is the most elusive of the three plays. We cannot be certain of its date--the card games mentioned were popular in Jacobean times and that is the extent of the internal evidence. We cannot be certain of its provenance--the Knave of Clubs tells us it is a Christmas entertainment (and the majority of college productions were written for holiday performance); Lily's Grammar is referred to and was a source, which suggests academic interests (as might its mythological subject matter); at best, we can only say it is likely a university play. And we cannot even be certain of its purpose--is it a veiled satire with political implications; an amateurish, somewhat silly, attempt at mock-heroic; or did an inept writer take himself seriously and imagine he was creating true tragicomedy?

---

[1] Hesiod, Theogony, trans. Norman O. Brown (New York: Bobbs-Merrill, 1953), p. 73.

[2] E. S. Taylor et al., The History of Playing Cards (Rutland, Vermont: Charles E. Tuttle and Company, 1973), p. 315.

V. ALL IN JEST: A CHRISTMAS MESSE

A Christmas Messe bears the date, 1619, on the first page of the manuscript. While this is undoubtedly the date of the copying of the manuscript, there is nothing to suggest that it is not also the date of the compositon. The manuscript is written in a clear and consistent hand and is remarkable in the rather fastidious quality the scribe displays. Only once (in line 563) is there a word scratched out to correct an error. One other time (in line 255) an error is corrected by carefully penning in the new reading below the error. In this latter case, one almost suspects the scribe had an aversion to unsightly blotches on his manuscript. In comparison to the manuscripts of our two preceding plays, the copying is extraordinary in its flawlessness, possessing none of the haphazardness which occasionally characterizes those manuscripts. Regrettably, much of the pain taken by the scribe of A Christmas Messe was for naught, for the legibility of the manuscript is greatly hampered by the seepage of ink through the paper. In some cases, the seepage nearly blots out whole words on the reverse side of the leaf. Were it not for the great care and distinction with which the scribe wrote, many lines would be next to impossible to read because of the ink seepage.

One is tempted to claim that the hand which wrote the manuscript is not the author's. There are no substantive emendations, save for the replacement of "Axell tree" for "Appletree" in line 255 (mentioned above), and this seems to be the result of miscopying. Indeed, since this emendation is so radical--"Appletree" makes absolutely no sense in the context, therefore rendering it unlikely that it was the author's first choice--it appears that this is only a miscopy. Further, it does not seem to be the sort of miscopy that an author/scribe would likely fall err to, since "Axell tree" is such a peculiar and distinctive reference. Of course, if the scribe is not the author, we are left with a somewhat puzzling question: Why would a relatively insignificant college play receive the attention of a scribal transcription? There are no ready and satisfactory answers.

That the play is of university origin, however, cannot be disputed. There is a very typical attack on the freshmen in lines 79-98, and a further comment on scholars appears in lines 569-70. Line 8 refers to "this goodly hall," undoubtedly the college hall where the play was to be performed, and it is quite clear that it was intended to be a Christmas production, perhaps the most characteristic purpose of all college plays. Also characteristic of college plays, there is no indication of the precise location of the performance. The play, along with the other two in the present edition, has been, in the past, ascribed to Cambridge. The ascription is puzzling. Cambridge seems to have favored comedies over tragedies, and Cambridge did produce far more plays than Oxford during the early seventeenth century, but these are no reasons for assigning all miscellaneous comedies to Cambridge. Gerald Bentley sees a relationship between the play and Thomas Randolph's _Salting_, which is a Cambridge play.[1] _The Salting_, a monologue existing only in a 316-line fragment, is written in iambic pentameter couplets and seems to be based on a college initiation custom. Salting consisted of a feast during which freshmen initiates, supervised by designated upperclassmen, competitively performed for the rest of the students. The specific nature of the performance seems not to have been prescribed, though it often took the form of an amateur theatrical. The _OED_ cites a 1644 source which reports that salting was "still used at Oxford," suggesting that Cambridge no longer practiced it (or at least that there is no record of such practice). But Randolph's play is certainly a Cambridge piece, and can be dated fairly closely to 1627. Consequently, if _A Christmas Messe_ is part of a salting, that fact alone would not establish its university of origin. Nevertheless, Bentley, perhaps out of convenience, assigns the play, as he does both _Heteroclitanomalonomia_ and _Gigantomachia_, to Cambridge.

But there are further, more substantial, reasons for doubting the Cambridge ascription. The fact is that _A Christmas Messe_ is found in a unique text bound in a commonplace book now in the Folger Shakespeare Library. It is the same collection which includes (in addition to the two other plays in this edition) _Periander_, a 1607 Oxford play. In the entire commonplace book there are no certain Cambridge plays, despite Bentley's statement to the contrary.[2] The point is that if we are to judge A Christmas Messe by its neighbors, there is no reason to assign it to Cambridge. Furthermore, there is some internal evidence suggesting its origin. In line 106, we find the term "sconct"--a university term referring to a fine imposed by the undergraduates on one of their own number for some breach of dining hall customs. And in line 203, we find a reference to "fly," which in this case refers to a cooks' festival. Both terms are designated by the OED as exclusive to Oxford. So, when all is considered, there seems to be much better reason to assign the play to Oxford than to Cambridge. Although our date is still insufficient to eliminate all doubt, Oxford has the better claim.

Belly, in the opening lines, quiets the audience and announces that his purpose is not what they might think, that is as "prologue to some mockshow," but rather simply to "find good cheare." But despite Belly's protests, we find much in the play that suggests a "mockshow"--or more precisely, a burlesque of heroic tragedy. The crux of the plot is the attempted usurpation by King Beefe of the right of King Brawne to be served up first at the traditional Christmas feast. The play is full of swaggering and bravado participated in by the two kings and their knights, Sir Pepper, Sir Vinigar, Lord Souce and Mustard. We are even treated to a token beauty, Queen Mincepy.

Brawne was the name given to the flesh of both pork and wild boar. It is probable that the latter is intended here, for in line 376 there is reference to the horn of King Brawne's father. Also, we may recall that the boar's head was a highly-prized dish at Renaissance Christmas feasts. Even twentieth-century Oxford has practiced the custom of ceremonially parading the boar's head into the dining hall to musical accompaniment prior to the holiday feasting. Efforts to uncover further contemporary references to a Christmas custom specifically requiring the roast pork or boar's flesh to precede the roast beef in Christmas dining etiquette have been unsuccessful. Although, it might be worth noting that pork was in general much favored over beef throughout the Middle Ages and the Renaissance--quite likely because the cooking methods produced extraordinarily tough and tasteless beef. There is, to be sure, nothing in the play to indicate that the boar's head ceremony is being referred to, but perhaps the audience would have naturally understood this. In the final analysis, we are left with only scanty clues on which to ponder the custom that this entire plot was built upon.

Both kings have their supporters who stand to gain from their respective leader's victory. King Beefe has by his side Sir Pepper and Sir Vinigar, as well as Queene Mincepy; King Brawne is supported by his son, Lord Souce, and Mustard. These are the more appropriate when we consider the great importance medieval and Renaissance cooking placed upon spices and sauces. Spices were used so heavily that they invariably camouflaged the principal ingredient of any dish, and there was no virtue in simple dishes. It is undoubtedly superfluous to point out that the two kings are accompanied by condiments suited to them. It is also appropriate that Queene Mincepy be at King Beefe's side--beef being one essential ingredient to true mince pie. Her presence in the play does little more than provide for some high-blown rhetoric in praise of her beauty--certainly a spoof on the legendary, if innocuous, royal beauties such as we might expect to find in _Tamburlaine_ or the spectacles of Kyd.

Aside from the obvious influences of these earlier Elizabethan tragedies, we can find, not surprisingly, reminiscences of classical Roman comedy. The two kings often seem thinly-disguised _miles gloriosi_, and their followers seem to waver between the roles of faithful servant and parasite (although they too have their chances to play the braggarts). It is also not completely far-fetched to see hints of the courtesan in Queene Mincepy. But much more than in the characterization, the Roman influence is reflected in the farcical elements.

Perhaps the most curious characters are those caught between--Bread, Salt, Trencher, Tablecloth, and Cushion. Much like helpless peasants in a dynastic quarrel, they are merely inconvenienced by the whole thing, and the outcome matters little to them. Like the Chorus of a classical tragedy, they appear on stage at the outset, emerge for occasional commentaries, then return to their appointed places. They do not converse with the principal characters, who seem quite unaware of their presence. In the vein of Kydian tragedy, however, they do supply something of an underplot paralleling the quarrel of the kings--

Tablecloth and Trencher vie for superiority, as do Salt and Bread. Cushion, much like the Cooke, acts as a mediator. We see here a variation on the Renaissance concept of order in the universe and the Great Chain of Being. Disruption at the top of society (the war between the two kings) results in disorder throughout the entire society (right down to Salt and Bread, Tablecloth and Trencher). Of course, nothing comes of this paralleling sub-plot, but even that parallels the main plot.

The characters most concerned about the fight between the two kings are, not unexpectedly, Belly and the Cooke. Belly is the typical Renaissance glutton; he cares not for custom or tradition, but only for his gratification. He is unhappy at the delay in dinner and is indignant when the audience refuses to take his plight seriously: "why doe yee looke after mee / I did not come for you to laugh at mee" (ll. 24-25). These lines may supply the only clue to costuming in the play. They anticipate laughter from the audience and suggest the character of Belly was to be costumed grotesquely. He was probably made to appear quite immense, assuming that the play was ever staged. He complains that his once proud enormity has shriveled from hunger: "I that was a tonne / In compasse, now am lesse then any ferkin? / See but how much there watnes to fill this jerkin / Oh how my gutts within my bulke doe rumble" (ll. 476-79).

It is the Cooke who takes the only real action in the play. He is "this greasy gull," reminding us of how dirty and wearisome the business of the Renaissance cook was. It is instructive to understand the prevailing attitude toward cooks during the period to fully appreciate the element of mock-heroic in A Christmas Messe. While some cooks attained, through their special talents, a degree of respectability in their masters' households, for the most part the office of the cook was low on the social scale. The job was messy and required hours of what often amounted to heavy labor. If at times the cook's creations were extraordinary works of art, more often they were the results of endless hours of mashing, grinding, chopping, beating, and overcooking. It indeed seems unlikely that we would today mistake a seventeenth-century kitchen for the scene of food preparation. The ill-tempered cook was proverbial, but considering his unpleasant task, we may easily understand how he got that way. The cook rarely made an appearance in the dining hall--doubtless because the sight of a sweaty, greasy and otherwise filthy cook could hardly have encouraged any appetite in the diners. But his prospects as a comic character in drama are obvious. It is interesing to note that a minor stock character in Roman comedy was the cook (cocus), who was used primarily to create laughter.[4] The cook's image in literature had not significantly changed in 2,000 years. So when this traditionally low comic character plays the arbitrator, furiously wielding his butcher knife as a staff of office, and returns order to the chaotic holiday feast, it is clear that we are dealing with a fanciful mock-heroic farce. He is the final ironic twist in the play--a sort of deus ex machina, not descending from the heavens to dispense justice, but emerging from the fiery hell of his kitchen to rid this play of its nonsense.

---

[1] See Fredson Bowers, "Thomas Randolph's 'Salting.'" Modern Philology, 39 (1942), 275-80.

[2] See specifically Bentley, V, 1342. Here Bentley is describing Gigantomachia as "perhaps a Cambridge product, as other items in the commonplace book are." Indeed, except for Jonson's "Christmas His Masque," which can claim no academic origins, and Sansbury's Periander, which can, from other sources, be ascribed to St. John's, Oxford, no other plays in the commonplace book have previously been examined thoroughly enough to establish their specific university origins.

[3] William E. Mead, The English Medieval Feast (Boston: Houghton Mifflin, 1931), p. 86.

[4] George E. Duckworth, The Nature of Roman Comedy (Princeton: Princeton University Press, 1971), p. 262.

PART 2: TEXTS

EDITORIAL POLICY

For the most part, the same editorial policy has been followed for all three plays. They do not present significantly different problems in editing. The interest in these plays is decidedly confined to the scholar of Renaissance drama and there seems little advantage in presenting an initial edition aimed at any but those with scholarly curiosity.

Consequently, in the absence of any previous edition of these plays, a modified diplomatic transcription has been chosen. Such typical Renaissance forms as "ff," "p," supralinear letters and supralinear lines indicating abbreviated forms are retained. On the other hand, no attempt has been made to reproduce the physical appearance of the manuscript leaves. The policy has been, in general, to note substantive scribal emendations and corrections, but not ordinary slips of the pen or fading of the ink. Thus, while the transcription is not purely diplomatic, the reader can have some notion as to how the scribe worked and what changes he thought fit to make. This is especially important when considering the first two plays, *Heteroclitanomalonomia* and *Gigantomachia*, where it is reasonable to assume that the authors were the scribes.

Unfortunately, the condition of the manuscript and the nature of the hands have not permitted very precise transcriptions at times. Capital letters, for example, are not always distinguishable from lowercase letters--particularly in the case of "w's," sometimes "k's," "n's," and "m's." When such letters occur as the initial letters in verse lines they have been capitalized, since that routine capitalization was fairly consistently practiced. Capitalization has not been tampered with when the scribe's intent can be unquestionably established, even though his purpose is not always clear. To establish authorial intent in the use of most punctuation would require a sixth sense. It is impossible to distinguish many commas from periods, many colons from semicolons, and so on. Fading ink and extraneous marks on the leaves do not make interpretation and transcription easy, nor do the casual punctuation practices of Renaissance scribes. The obvious marks have not been altered, of course. When an editorial judgment concerning accidentals has been required, the editing has been done silently. When the accidentals may confuse the substantive meaning, footnotes have been provided to offer a clearer reading.

In all cases, the footnotes are intended to indicate editorial emendations, explicate obscure passages, and translate Latin expressions. They are not intended to expound any critical interpretation or to intrude upon the reader in any way.

HETEROCLITANOMALONOMIA

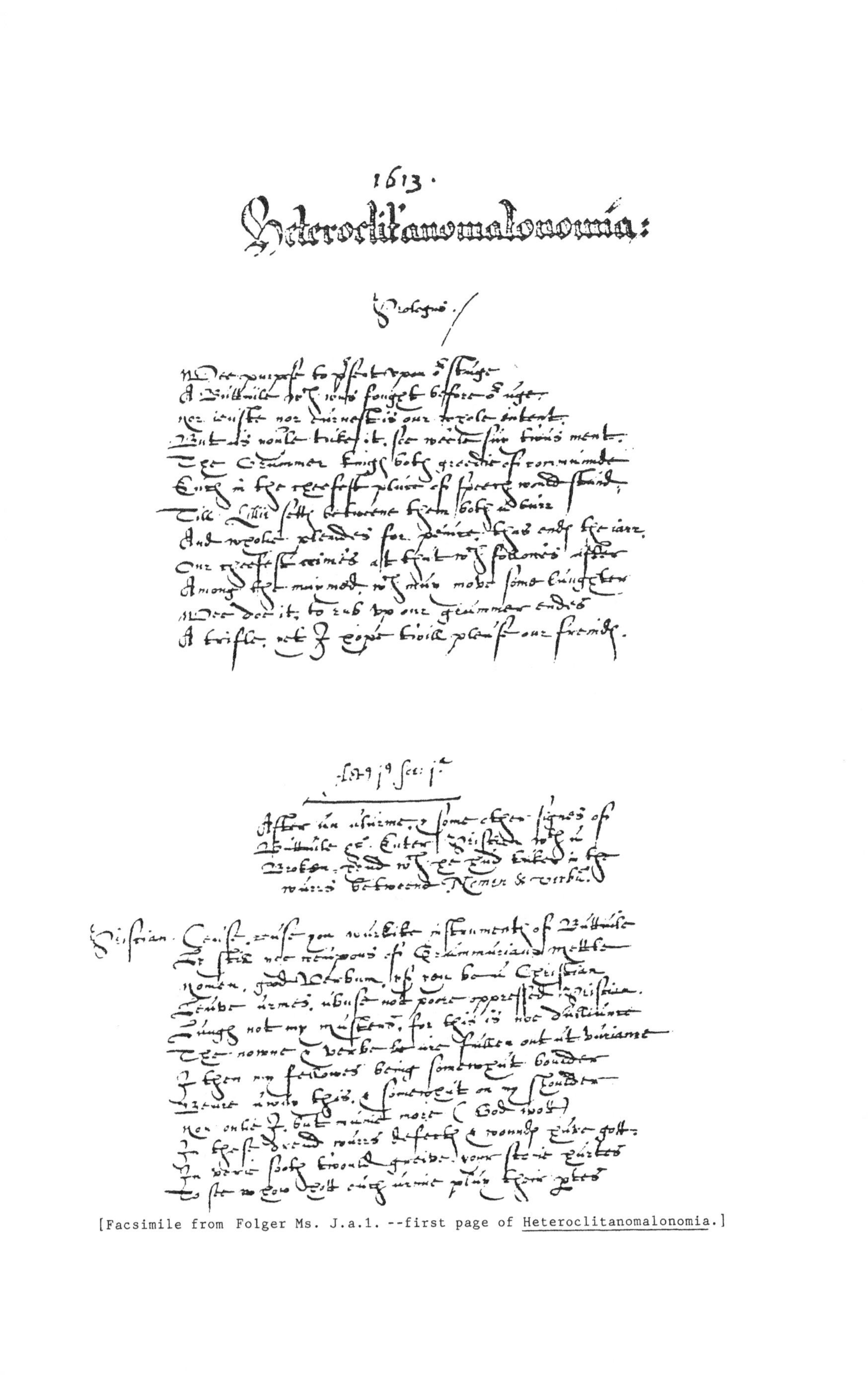

1613.

Heteroclitanomalonomia:

Prologus.

Actus 1us Scena 1a

[Facsimile from Folger Ms. J.a.1. --first page of Heteroclitanomalonomia.]

[Prologue]

1613

Heteroclitanomalonomia

Prologus

Wee purpose to p^{r}sent upon o^{r} stage
A Battaile wch was fought before o^{r} age;
Nor ieaste nor earnest is our whole intent,
But as you'le take it, soe we'ele say t'was ment.
The Grammer Kings both greedie of commande
Each in the cheefest place of speech would stand;
Till Lillie setts betweene them both a barr
And wholie pleades for peace, thus ends the iarr.
Our cheefest rime's at that wch followes after
Among the maymed, wch may move some laughter
Wee doe it, to rub up our grammer endes
A trifle, yet I hope t'will please our freinds.

---

10 Lillie] William Lily (1468?-1522), the English grammarian and author of one of the most influential Latin grammars, which came to be known as <u>Lily's Grammar</u>.

12 rime's] The manuscript is not clearly legible; an initial letter seems to be blotted, suggesting a scribal error and attempted correction. There are many such instances in the manuscript. If this is not assumed to be the case, the reading would seem to be "crime's"--but all sense is lost on such a reading.

14 rub . . . endes] That is, "brush up on our Latin inflections and so on." The play is full of references to inflected forms of Latin grammar, or the "endes" of Latin words.

[I:1]

Act 1 Sce: 1

After an alarme, & some other signes of Battaile [gr]. Enter Priscian wth a Broken-head wch he had taken in the warrs betweene Nomen & Verbū.

Priscian: Cease, cease you warlike instruments of Battaile
Ly still yee weapons of Grammarians mettle
Nome, good Verbum, yf you be a Christian
Leave armes, abuse not poore oppressed Priscian.
Laugh not my masters, for this is noe dalliance
The nowne & verbe are fallen out at variance
I then my fellowes being somewhat boulder
Beare away this, & somewhat on my shoulder.
Nor onlie I, but manie more (God wott)
In these dread warrs defects & wounds have gott.
In verie sooth t'would greive your stonie hartes
To see how hott each armie play their ptes
ffirst both the kinds doe gather up their Numbers

---

18 *gr*] The identification and meaning of these two letters are obscure. The initial letter seems almost certainly to be *g*, which greatly narrows the possibilities and obscures the meaning even more. Since this is a stage direction, we might suspect some theatrical abbreviation, but none which is logical comes to mind. Perhaps something like "Battaile gr[ound]" was intended or it may be a peculiar rendition of "etc." or something similar. The scribal hand was often inconsistent and careless.

29-30 Nor . . . gott] These grammar wars, of course, allegorically explain all the irregularities of the language.

And each their Captaines from their Cowards sunders.
The articles as *Hic*, *haec*, *hoc* and others
Begin the Battaile sparing not their Brothers.
To them three persons of King Verbum's side
As ego, tu, and ille soone replied,
Then the declensions in their severall rankes
Wth Coniugations 'gins to play their prankes.
The Gerunds & the Supines they stand by
To drowne wth drumbes & ffifes the maymed's cry;
Verbes wch have lost their limbes *quam plurima dantur*,
Ft quae deficiunt genere adiectiva notantur.
Heare lies a p̱fect-tence of Verbum' troupe.
And on the other side yf you would stoope,
You might take up a hundred thousand Cases;
There standeth ffero making crabbed faces.

---

34 Captaines . . . Cowards] The meaning seems clear--the kings are separating the "men from the boys"--although the appellations are curious. The author may have been conscious of the effect of the alliteration, and he may have been thinking of the Latin roots of the two words: "captain" is derived from the Latin for "head," "coward" from the Latin for "tail." The pairing may not be as peculiar as we might initially think.

43-44 *quam* . . . *notantur*] The Latin may be translated: "are found to be very many,/ And those which are adjectives lack their own gender." The reference is to the participles which function as adjectives, and, of course, in Latin an adjective adopts the gender of the noun which it modifies.

48 crabbed faces] Probably a reference to the verb *fero*'s extraordinarily irregular principal parts, which are so distorted they do not remotely resemble the root.

ffor his lost pfect-tence, an other lies
Lame of his leggs. *Caecus* he wants his eies.
Volo crowdes valiantlie into the presse
But strayte (alas) returns imperativelesse
Dice wth speeches thinking to prevaile
Comes back poore Dic cut shorter by the taile.
Soe Vis the nowne although he thought no harme
Yet in this skirmish lost his giving arme.
Fumus he smoak't fort', what with shott & thunder,
He never since could find his plurall number.
The Guns so bounc't in *Quidam's* eares & face
Hee's thick of hearing in his *Calling* case.
What more? some Verbes grew hoarse that wth their noyse
Some lost their *Active* some their passive voyce.
In these hott warres, where neyther Verbe nor nowne
Saw their owne fellowes groveling on the ground,
The Adiectives wth their substantives did buffett,

---

50 *Caecus*] The Latin noun for "blind."

51 Volo] The verb meaning "to wish," which has no proper imperative mood.

55 Vis] Strength or force.

57 Fumus] Smoke, a noun not regularly used in the plural (see line 4).

59 *Quidam*] As an indefinite pronoun, *quidam* would properly have no vocative or "Calling" case (see line 60).

And I wth ꝑting them was soundlie cuffed.

An alarme. See heere the signe. But harke, Gerundes in Dum
Doe sound their Trumpetts. Supins beate their drumbe.
O fie upon these warres, & fowle ambition
Each ageinst other, both ageinst poor Priscian,
This is no time nor place for me to stay.
The nownes & Verbes draw neere. I must away.

Exit.

Act 1 Sce: 2

Enter Oratio held by Nomen on one arme &
by Verbum on the other and after them Lillie

Verb: Oratio is mine, my handes the first did light on her.
Nomen thou wert not best to cast one sight on her.

Nom: Peace Verbū, peace, thou nothing art but worde
Renowned Nowne shall gett her wth his sworde.

Orat: Houlde both yor hands. Oratio speakes in teares,

66] In Guarna's Bellum Grammaticale, Priscian suffers similar wounds. See the introduction for a discussion of the treatment of Priscian.

67 Gerundes in Dum] That is, the accusative case of the gerund, which ends in -dum in Latin. The same phrase can be found in Lily's Shorte Introduction of Grammar.

68 Supins] As a verb form, the Latin supine functions very much like the English infinitive, but with noun endings; the supines would be in that same limbo between noun and verb as the gerunds.

75 Oratio] The mastery of Latin oratory would have been the crowning achievement of every Renaissance scholar; the personification of oratory as the desired queen is therefore appropriate.

ffor be you sure, that such a death of Wordes
As this your battaile every howre affords
Must needs hurte me, the world was never better
Then when we did enioy our servant *Caeter*.
Whome ye have slaine, wth manie of his order,
All wch ar dead, whats this but open murther!
Yf you goe forward as you have begun,
All Grammer-Land will quicklie be undon.
I feele that Barbarisme nighe approaches,
When our best sub̄tes all doe halte in crotches.
Some loose their legges, their armes yea bodies, and some
Withall do loose their lives, thinke you this hansome.
Decree a peace; of you this onlie seeke I

---

84 hurte] The letter *r* has been inserted presumably by the scribe.

85 servant *Caeter*] The letters "sev" are scratched out before "servant," apparently only a misspelling of that word. Caeter's name may be derived from *caeterus*, the "rest" or "remaining," the term used by Lily when he writes of exceptions to rules (Heteroclites, for example), very much as English grammars do. An English example is the familiar "i before e, *except after c*." Latin grammar contains numerous exceptions to the rules. It is the inability to acknowledge exceptions which has brought Nomen and Verbum into conflict. Caeter was therefore a useful servant of grammar.

91 sub̄tes] The supralinear bar throughout the manuscript indicates omitted letters. The word here is not a standard abbreviation, but "subjects" seems to be intended, and it certainly makes sense in the context.

<u>Praest enim regredi, quam mala coepta sequi.</u>
[Nom:] Il'e pawne my creddit, yf thou wilte beleeve me;
Il'e doe what eare I may for to releeve thee.
But Il'e not loose my precious prize, thats flatt;
What's mine is mine, & I will have but that.
Verbū: Whats thine proud nowne, base, lowlie Beggers peasant,
I would I could but once espie thee sease on't.
Orat: Leave of these Lowsie Beggars yf you love me,
The very name of Peasant much doth move me.
Lillie: Since she is his & yours, but wholie neyther,
T'is best you both should for a respite leave her
Or both possesse her but in quiett manner,
You doe not well, thus for to hange upon her.
Please you to lend yor eares, you strait shall see,
Some articles to wch both shall agree.
Nom: Content saie I not that I feare to combat
Wth that same Verbū, whom If I come at,
Ile teach him how to meddle wth my Wenches
He hath enough to doe wth moods & tences.
Ver: And I agree for this my mistres love
Not yours, an other time these words shall ꝑve.
Lillie: Why now you deale like Kings to end this toyle
Be pleased therefore for to sitt a while,

---

95 <u>Praestat . . . sequi</u>] "It is better indeed to retreat than to follow bad beginnings."

116 <u>toyle</u>] An illegible letter, apparently the result of scribal correction, is blotted after the <u>t</u>.

Oratio in the middle like a mother:
Nomen on one side, Verbū on the other

Ora: Speake then (grave Lillie) as a wise man should doe,
Where be these compositions, say what would yee?

Lillie: For the due ioyning of wordes in construction it is to be understanded, that in Latine Speech there be three concordes, the first betweene the nominative case and the verbe, the seacond betweene the substantive and the adiective, the third betweene the antecedent and the relative.

Ora: Why? this is true, but now we aske of thee
How may we make these enemies agree.

Lillie: The last 2 Concords doe agree alreadie
Although the nowne & verbe be somewhat headie
About thee Queene Oratio, as it seemes;
Wherefore in this my iudgm^{t} fittest deemes,
That yf yee doe consider Nomens case,
Why, then the Verbe shall take the cheefest place.
But yf yee doe respect the Persons, then
I take the nownes to be the better man.
Thus both shall Raigne but at their severall seasons
In an oration for thaforesaid reasons.
How like Oratio this devise for peace?

122-37] This entire speech by Lillie is taken verbatim from William Lily's *Shorte Introduction of Grammar* (1567), sig. C4^{r}. (This edition of Lily will be referred to hereafter.)

Orat: Full well (good Lillie) doe they Nomen please?

Nom: They doe, & doubtles he were verie crosse
That would not lett wise Lillies sentence passe.
How please they Verbū? Ver: all as well as may be,
I nee'r sawe better articles then they be.
Be you but pleasd' in publick wee'le reveale them,
And with our hand, & privie Signett seale them.

Ora: We all consent, Lillie lead on the way
We meane to aske the next schoole leave to play.

Ver: Which being done, dread Queene) I will returne,
To comfort those wch in these warres doe morne
And send backe trustie Participles armie,
W^{ch} he eare long will have ꝓvided for me.

<u>Exeunt omnes</u>.

149] The most probable meaning of this line is "We mean to ask permission of the next school to perform our play there." Volo, in line 465 below, refers to going about "to all the Country schooles." These references raise an interesting possibility: that this play was intended for presentation by itinerant actors before various grammar schools. We do know that college players often found themselves performing outside the university precincts, but they were usually uninvited and often only goading the townspeople who were perennially the butts of university satire. A true public service performance would be uncharacteristic, to be sure, even if it were for profit, which is even more unlikely. But it is a consideration which should not be overlooked. See the introduction for a further consideration.

150 dread Queene)] The initial parenthesis was omitted by the scribe, who apparently intended to enclose this direct address.

Chorus

Wee'le be as neat, as you know who before us.
I'le tell you Sirs, our play shall have a Chorus.
And I am he, I speake it with an Emphasis
My hoopes expound my name it is Paranthesis.
The eplilouge, & prolouge--they doe stand,
Like these same Semicircles in my hand.
W^{ch} thus encloses wth their Semimoone,
Our needeles sports, wch well may be undon--
But to my part. the kings as you have seen't,
Are freinds, the Compositions are in print.
But now the nownes & verbes are fallen in,
Anomalaes & Hetroclites begin.
Sitt heere a while, & you shall see some sport,
W^{ch} they shall make, then laugh, & thanke us for't.
Yet stay a little, lett me not forget you,
One thing I have, for wch I must entreat you

156] The reference in this line was probably to some well-known fastidious scholar in the audience. Such esoteric gibes were typical of university drama and the inclusion of this gibe does not necessarily negate the speculation that the play may have been intended for a variety of audiences (see note to line 148 above). The reference may be to one of the players, for example, or perhaps to someone who functioned as a faculty sponsor or advisor. It is, at any rate, an "in joke" with the originally-intended cast.

167 Anomalaes & Hetroclites] An anomaly in Latin grammar is a verb conjugated irregularly; a heteroclite is a noun "declined otherwise then the bare rules of declension doe require" (Lily, sig. Il^{v}). These two groups are the principal combatants in the play and they give their names to the formidable title.

[II:1]

Pray lett them twange their instruments a little,
Till I am tyrd'e, for I play Participle.

Act 2^{d} Sce: 1

Enter Participiū sol̄: wth two l̄res.

Par: The Grammer fallen at odds. this newes is sad.
I feare wth p̲ticiple t'will goe bad. Legit l̄ras.
To his right trusty subiect Don Pedro
Participio inhabiting in Accedence Allie
beyond great Possum neare to the abode

---

173 tyrd'e] Attired; from the chorus we are able to infer no small amount of information about the performance (or intended performance). There was to be music between the acts, and the properties and costumes were apparently somewhat detailed. It is also instructive to note the double part played by Participle. The need to economize on players may give strength to the hypothesis that the play was intended as a traveling production for grammar schools (see the note to line 148 above), a circumstance which might account for the limited number of actors. Of course, it may also mean that the actor who played Participle and Parenthesis simply wanted to do both parts--and even more importantly that he had a hand in the writing. The audience is addressed as "Sirs," which certainly designates it as an academic audience which would have contained no women. (Of course, such an audience as one would find at the Inns of Court would have been male-dominated also, but the rest of the internal evidence seems to overrule any but academic provenance.) But most certain of all, the chorus clearly indicates that the play was written with production in mind and not merely as a literary or pedagogical exercise.

174 two l̄res.] Two letters; one from Nomen and one from Verbum, both entreating Participle's support. Only the letter from Verbum is read aloud.

178] The residence of Participle in Accidence (that is, inflection) Alley near Possum, Eo and Queo, all verbs, perhaps suggests his first allegiance should be to Verbum. This is what Verbum thinks, at any rate.

of Signior Eo and Queo.
I know thou art not ignorant honourable Participle with what insolence, and hawtiness of minde Poeta king of the Nownes hath made an insurrection, and how rashlie he presums ageinst the Law of Verbes to usurpe the supremacie in an Oration, in so-much that wee are compelled to take up armes though very un-willinglie ageinst him to beate downe his pride and save o^{r} owne honour, wherfore being you know full well how much ye are beholden to us, as for your tence and signification you should performe an action befitting your fidelity yf you would praeserve the common opinion we have allwaies had of you from the beginning by adioyning your bandes and your salfe to ours not only for the praeservation of us, but also for your owne safetie, of which you should have cause to despaire should our empire be once over-throwne farwell, and hasten thy coming as thou art able.

Amo Verbū

Stand toot'stout Nownes much honour may you merrit

---

183 Peota] This was the name originally given by Guarna to the Noun King. Hutten used the name in his dramatic version of *Bellum Grammaticale*, but this is the only use of that nomenclature in this play. It does demonstrate the author's knowledge of these predecessors.

200 Amo] The name Guarna gave to the Verb king (see the note to line 185).

To gett Oratio & proud Verbū ferrit.
Fight on stout Verbū, noe lesse mayst thou win,
To gett oratio, & beat Nomen in.
Strike on both p̲ties, heer's none will forbid it,
Brave be mine honour, this is Grammers creddltt.
I'me for you both, but yet indeed for neyther,
Though I love you, beleeve me I had rather
Plesure my selfe then both. Then Verbe & Nomen
Learne this of me, t'is best for you to know men,
before you trust them, t'is a common Proverbe.
Doest thinke, that I'le neglect my p̲fitt? no Verbe.
They write to me to ioyne my Bands to theirs
And each of them the losse of Kingdome feares;
I'me glad of that, when two extreames do strive,
Then is the middle very like to thrive.
And yet because they shall not know my meanings,
A few Il'e send them of my courser gleanings,
The Verbes p̲happes a few neutropassivaes,
Lest they mistrust me, (oh thei're p̲illous slye knaves)
The nownes some Toyes wch end in Tor & *Trix*.

---

219 neutropassivaes] This is the medieval term for a semi-deponent Latin verb. A deponent verb has a passive form, but an active meaning, while a semi-deponent verb is normal in the present system, but deponent in the perfect. The term "neutropassive" is used by Lily in his *Grammar*; its appropriateness here seems to be that such verbs present particular difficulties in their conjugation, explaining their label, "p̲illous slye knaves," in line 220. See Lily, sig. D2^{r}.

ffor such slight things noe politician stickes.
I have enough to serve my turne & more,
Why, I can number halfe an hundred skore,
As those in *Ans, Ens, Tus, Sus, Xus, Rus*, and *Dus*
My souldiers doe in number passe the Sandust.
And more then that, proud Nomen do but thwart y^{u} us
Wee'le rayse the spiritt of our long dead mortuus.
Well, well, I will be king at least, beshrow me,
But neyther nowne nor Verbe can keepe it for me.
Enter Verbū, Volo, fero, Dic.

Act 2 Sce: 2

Ver: Since wars be donne, lett $ev^{r}y$ of our nation,
Betake him to his proper habitation.
Par: How now king Verbū? Hah? what fled? Now wellaway,
How goes the warrs, hath nomen bare the Bell away.
Ver: Why they be done; I scarce had seald' my letter,
When Lillie ioyn'd us freinds. Par: Better, & better
Thus while I make my selfe of all soe sure, [aside]

---

225 *Ans . . . Dus*] A similar list of terminats may be found in Guarna's *Bellum Grammaticale*.

226 Sandust] The meaning is, of course, grains of sand, numberless.

227 proud] This word was first written after *more*, then scratched out and moved to this location. Such a syntactical change might suggest the authorial hand.

228 mortuus] This Latin participle meaning "dead" seems to have two functions here, and one is to facilitate the rhyme. Its meaning is best explained by regarding the expression as a personification of dead words, archaisms.

I'me guld'e of all, who can such fals endure?
But ar the warrs brake up? I'me glad, beleeve me.
ffor both yor sakes, that onlie doth releive me.
Had it not binne for you, the Participle
Voyde of all helpe, had still remaind' a Cripple.
Yf you had chanct' to loose yor domination;
Where should I had tence or signification?
Had Nowne untimelie fell in that dissention,
What should I done for gender, case, declension?
Yf both had died, my dammage had binne bigger,
Where should I had my number or my figure?
All wch considered, sure he were not worthie,
Such kindenes, who would not be carefull for the.
Ver: I know you're carfull, & I thanke you fort'--
Although your kindnes at this time came short;
I must impute it to my too late sending
And not in anie wise to yor offending.
But I am glad you did a while with-hold yours,
ffor had I had a verie few more souldiers,
All Nomens troupes had binne of life bereft,
There had not then one Adiective beene left.
Par: Me thinks that you are reasonably tamed
As far as I see, manie of your are maymed.
Ver: T's true, t'was our hard fortune, & o^{r} fate
That thus massacred them; But say, relate,
How ev^{r}y wound to each of you befell

And by what mischeefe? Dic: ffaith' I cannott tell,
But as I'me Dic, I in the wars could never thrive
ffor there I lost the tayle of my Imperative.
I as my use was, when I see one come,
Turning my Back, a Nowne strooke of my Bum.
Volo: And I poore Volo being somewhat willful,
Was though I say't my selfe not quite unskillfull.
And yet my iackett some Nowne had a pull at,
My Passive voyce was struck of wth a Bullett.
Fero: But silly ffero bore the brunt of all,
There did my pfect-tence untimelie fall,
But yet I hope your Lordships war-munition
Will for our labours give us restitution.
Oh to be pfect is an happenesse,
And to be tenced is to me no lesse
Then that I may be pfected, & tenced,
Let me (I pray) with your rewards be fenced.
Dic: But to goe taylesse is a worse disgrace,
ffor shame I dare not looke you in the face

---

283 taylesse] Above this word in the manuscript another hand has written what appears to be "tail-esse." The intervention of this annotator, apparently of the eighteenth century or later, occurs occasionally throughout the text. In line 284, the same hand has transcribed "shame" correctly, but in line 285, "Raskall" has been mistakenly transcribed "skillfull."

O that same Raskall cald *Apocope*
Could not he bange me, but must take my *E*?
Wherfore my Lord, my elboe daylie itches,
Hoping you will restore my long lost breeches.

Volo: My dammages (dread King) you knew before,
Denie not then my losses to restore.

Ver: How now (my freinds) for recompences sute yee?
I hope that you have donne, but whats yor dutie.
Yet in Rewarding woonds I would not lagger.
But that these warrs have made me quite a bagger.
Wherfore be answerd', may the matter scan not
ffor I am forc'd indeed to say I cannott.
Seeks for rewards? now all my moods defend me,
I'me allmost mad; Good Participle 'tende me.

Exeunt Verbū & Particip.

Act 2 Sc: 4

Dic: Is this a recompence for all our warres?
Is this a salve fit for soe daunderous scarrs?
I'le tell you Sirs, although I make noe grudging,
Well may you thinke, I take the same in dudgen.
Thats stird my collor much, & can you blame me?

---

285 *Apocope*] This is the grammatical term for the loss of sounds or letters at the end of a word. Apocope deprives "dice" of its final "e" in its root form in Latin grammar.

294 bagger] Miser; presumably his war losses have necessitated frugality.

300 Sc: 4] The scribe inaccurately numbered this scene, which is, of course, the third.

304 dudgen] Anger; resentment.

Whie; losse of Tayle it cannot chuse but shame me.
Volo: Indeed thats much, but my commaunding moode
His taile, head, bodie, all all ar drencht in bloud.
How may I storme for this same losse of mine,
W^{ch} in the warrs did all commaund resigne?
But Verbū I will make thee know (thou Base theife)
I will not beare those wrongs. I have noe Passive.
Fero: High hoe, I'me active passive both together,
Yet to say truth, I ꝑfect am in neyther.
I want that tence, yet simple though that I am,
I'le goe to Verbum, once againe I'le try him,
Yf he will make me restitution for it,
If he denie it, I must needs goe borrow it.
Dic: ffy, fy, noe ffero, t'is a shame to borrow,
I'le make him give the one before to morrow:
Be ruld by me, wee'le trounce that thanklesse Verbū,
I'le tell you Sirs, I'le make this same a deare Bum.
Hee'd better brake his neck from of a Steeple,
Then usd' us thus, t'is that same Participle,
W^{ch} like a Hang-on or a fflattring Parrasite.
Getts all from us. he'ele still be sure to tarry by't.
Fero: Hee's tarried by it so long, that now the whorsone

---

306 Whie] Why; the interjection.

327] The mysterious annotator mentioned above has penned into the margin "tarried," a correct transcription of the second word in this line. An illegible word has been scratched from the manuscript before whorsone. This seems to be another scribal correction.

Hath gott into his fingers every Person:
My moode Imp̱ative it wants the first
For wch to ask Verbe yet I never durst.
Because I knew he'd given him so manie,
That now for me to spare he had not anie.
Well well I knew the time, when t'was a fashion,
That ev^{r}y nowne of whatsoever nation,
Should be the third, now they ar not affeard,
To be the first, the seacond, or the third.
Nay more, this was confirmed by p̱clamation,
Cryd' in the market-place by Evocation,

Volo: This must be lookt' to. ffellowes letts be wise,
Yf Volo might be heard, I'de you advise
To take up armes ageinst our carelesse kinge
We'ele make him know that Beetles have a stinge.

Fero: ffight with our King? is that a thing so little?
Ile tell the Volo, that I am no bettle.
Nor will I take up armes ageinst our King.

Enough of the deleted word is ascertainable to indicate it may have been an alternate spelling of "whorsone" (perhaps, "Horson"). Such spelling corrections occur throughout the play.

327-38] This entire speech by Fero is, of course, based on Latin Grammar. Lily tells us ". . . . all nounes, pronounes, & participles be of ye third person" (sig. B2^{r}) (that is, all pronouns he has not already assigned to the first and second persons). Therefore, the meddling by Participle and the nouns into the first and second persons is both unnatural and a transgression. Fero, as a verb and, thus possessing all three persons (except in his imperative mood), is understandably indignant.

So I my selfe may to worse mischeefe bring.
As I am ffero, I have borne some losses,
And ear' I'le do't, will beare farr greater crosses.
Besids whereas King Verbum did denie me,
Perhaps he did it onlie for to trie me.
Had I my pfect-tence, then thou should'st see,
My noble Vole I would be for thee.

Dic: But give me leave (good ffero) I beseech thee,
In this case I am able for to teach thee.
Think'st thou to gett thy tence againe? (o wissard)
Take this from me: to gett from Verbū t'is hard.
Wert' in my case, thou should'st not go to ask a Tence.
Wee'd quicklie ferritt Verbum from the accedence.
Wer't in my case, quoth I? why I am worse,
I have more reason Verbū for to curse.
But heer's an Anvill, wch yf I can hammer,
Ile quicklie set on fire Will Lillies Grammer.

Volo: I am resolvd'. yf fortune doe but favour us,
Proud Verbe ear' long shall leave to triumph over us.
Let us turne out-Lawes, & who ear' we meate,
We'ele rifle them, be it in open streete.

Fero: Why then I see I must beare what betide me,

358] Before _ferritt_ letters which seem to be "fett" are blotted, apparently another scribal error.

366] The word "him" is blotted after _rifle_. Such substantive changes as this and the one in line 382 below may indicate that the manuscript is in the authorial hand.

I'le follow them. Ill ffortune fall beside me.

<u>Exeunt omnes</u>.

Actus 2 Sce: 5

Enter Absurdo laughing.

ffaith don Absurdo, th'art a noble Lad
Thy wares will utter, be they ne'ere so bad.
But shall I say, what heere I have to sell?
Let me put downe my pack, & then Ile tell.
It was not long since I did understand
Of the great difference in Grammer-Land
Betwene the Nowne & Verbe upon wch muttring
I did presume my wares would want no uttering.
I laded then an Asse wth all such wordes
As this whole Grammer-Land no where affords;
Wth out-worne phrases & ould coniugations,
Now some young startups, following still new fashions
Would needs se all my wares, each for them seeks
Nay more; they faine would learne Absurdoes tricks;
And speake his speech, but marke what follow'd after,
Pray understand me, for t'is worth the laughter.
An olde, grey-bearded bonnd-head father came,

383] The word "new" is scratched out before "young" --a substantive change not uncommon in the manuscript (see the introduction)

388 grey-breaded bonnd-head] Originally, the scribe had written "grey-headed" then corrected it to "-bearded." "Bonnd-head" is something of a mystery, but the <u>OED</u> does record a "bondehede," a combination of "bound" and "head" meaning "bondage." It is not unlikely that

[II:5]

I thinke they cald' him Priscian. yes, the same.
You may not speake (quoth he) such Barbarous phrases.
A word ill spoken oft great tumults rayses.
No sooner spake he, but a moodie Squire
Amongst the companie sett all on fire
Wth these his speeches, lent him such a Clap,
As made the bloud come trickling downe his cap.
Absurd, Absurd cryde he, now others followed,
Crying & pelting him, I whoopt' & hallowed,
My Asse he kikt', my wares were all untied,
Fresh companie came. Absurd the ould man cry'de,
You hurt me, you shall awnswer't ere be long sir,
I hurt ye not quoth I, you doe me wrong sir,
But then thought I, tis best for me to leave them
Soe tooke this part, & lest I should deceave them
That were my Customers, there I left my Asse
Glad that I scaped soe, & thus did passe;
As for the Beast, my customers may ride him,
Soe for my scattred wares lett them devide 'm.
This only I reserv'd, wch yf I cry it.
I know that manie heere about will but it.
    Who wants a number, case, or gender

"bonnd-head" is a corruption of this term and that it refers to the bondage of convention which has come to characterize Priscian, the ancient authority against whom the real thrust of the rebellion is aimed. This would also explain the symbolism of the grey beard. On the other hand, "bound-head" may be intended (see lines 394-95).

Of anie nowne I can it render.
Who ever lacks a maimde verbes mood,
Come unto me I'le make it good;
Come along ye Ladds see what yee lack
And ease absurdo of his pack.
But stay (Absurd) heere Customers are none.
All civell are, thy harborers are gone.
Sure, sure I mist my way. I may not tarry heere.
I must to Ignorance, I am his Carrier.
But soft, who are those fellowes that are lurking
Each of them beares some writing on his ierkin.

Act: 2 Sce: 6

Enter to Absurdo Volo, fero, dic.

Fero: Say ffellowes, han't we gott us pretty prizes?
Volo: Yes, lett's take heed, lest that the Country rises,
ffor we have made shrowd uprores. Fero: o 'tis best,
Till we be ꝑfect, few shall take their rest,
Poore Tulo he lies breathles voyd of sences,
But I am glad I ha' gott his ꝑfectences;

---

412 maimde] This word is underscored and, in the margin, glossed as "maim'd" by the same hand which entered the glosses already mentioned.

426 shrowd] Shrewd; with the meaning of vexatious, dangerous.

428 Tulo] This is a medieval form of "fero" no longer current in Renaissance times. Remnants of the older form can still be seen in the perfect active indicative stem of "fero"--"tuli," which is referred to in line 429.

Thus have we somewhat. Dic: yea, you may be glad,
But honest dic amongst you fareth bad,
I am a curtaill still. Volo: soft who comes hither?
Abs: A foe or freind to out-lawes, choose ye whether.
My name's Absurdo famous through most nations,
Fro bringing up strange orders, & new fashions.
Dic: Wherefore cam'st thou to this place? Abs: don't you see?
Only because the place came not to me.
Vol: Welcome in faith (good Don) but pree'the tell us,
What busines ha'st? Abs: I see you're merry fellowes;
Your letters terme ye Out'lawes, your ar well mett,
I'le tell you what; poore Priscian wants a helmett,
What betweene you & me & such as we be
All out-lawes, all unrulie, nee're will he be
Without the Red-worme crawling downe his pate;
Soe I with other youngsters usd him late,
And hither fled I. Fero: O'but heer's no tarrying,
All heare are freinds to Priscian, nothing varying
From his good orders; Some there are that care not
What they doe speake or doe, seeke them, & feare not,

---

432 curtaill] This noun form, meaning anything that has been shortened, was common in the sixteenth and seventeenth centuries.

440 your] While this is the correct manuscript reading, it seems apparent that "you" was intended.

444 Red-worme . . . pate] This rather vivid image suggest the blood streaking down Priscian's head and somewhat resembling a red worm.

As country Lobbes, & clonnes that have noe knowledge,
Rude Pedagogs & Newcomes of the Colledge.
Thei're they best chapman; we must hence away.
Ab: Tell me before you goe where did you lay.
Dead Tuloes furniture, I should use his moodes.
Fero: Those you shall find heere by the Errours woods.
What we have left of his (Absurdo) take it.
We did pvide our selves of what we lacked.
Ab: Thankes (good Anomalaes) I must goe seeke them,
Tulo Tulebam? who can choose but like them?
Farwell unto you all. Volo: the like to you.
Dic: Well, well my masters, heer's a deale a doe
ffor moodes & tences & such other triftles,
But I poore dic must goe away wth nifles
But now what to be donne? you have yor tooles.
Lett's goe about to all the Country schooles
Set them a gag to break that head of Priscians,
They have noe knowledge of yor new additions.

---

450 Lobbes, & clonnes] Bumpkins and clowns.

451 Newcomes] Newcomers; presumably the college freshmen.

461 deale a doe] Commotion, trouble, fuss.

462 triftles] This seems to be only a misspelling of "trifles." It is obviously intended to rhyme with "nifles" and there is no record of such a variant spelling of "trifles."

463 nifles] Trifles.

465 Country schooles] See the note to line 149 above.

Stand toot' stout Brothers. since we are anomalaes
Noe rule shall governe us, I say we'ele ha' noe Lawes.

Fero: Very good counsell, since we are anomalaes,
I say wee'le goe at Randum, we will ha' noe Lawes.

Exeunt omnes.

Chorus.

Now I resume ageine Parenthesis,
Come for to tell you what is ment by this
Wch in the second act you saw before,
In livelie manner acted, & noe more.
ffirst then the Verbes would have their losse restord
Having repulse they thretten fire & sowrde.
These verbes be pillous Rouges, for in a spleene
They kill & slay, the like was never seene.
ffero meets Tulo voyd of all defence
Knocks him downe dead & steales his pfect-tence.
Noe lesse doth Volo to some Verbe or other
And takes up Vis & velle, but their Brother,
Poore Dic I meane, getts nought at all amonge them
Thus strive they to avenge him that doth wrong them:
But as they goe, they meet wth Don Absurd,
They tell him of their prize, who at a worde,
Goes backe, & finds the ffurniture by chance,

---

480 Rouges] Certainly a misspelling for Rogues.

485 Vis & velle] *Vis* is the Latin for "force" or "violence"; *velle* is the present infinitive form of *volo*.

And selles them to his chapman Ignorance.
Thinke that the Nownes doe play like Raks wth in,
Sitt heere & see, now doe the game begin.
Yet for a while, lett musick make you merry
To ease our actors wch be almost wery.

Act 3 Sc: 3

Enter Vis, fumus, Aliquis.

Vis: Nomen for peace entreats, from war dehorts,
Thretning dred punishment to us (consorts)
If that we treat but wth our lookes of fight,
Soe direfull is it in his kinglie sight,
Then I the Captaine of his warlick traynes
Hoping that he would poyse his daungerous maynes,
With kind rewards, unto the court repayrd.
Thinking full little how I should have fay'rde.

---

492 Raks] Rakes.

496 Sc: 3] A manuscript error. It, of course, should read "Scene 1."

503 poyse . . . maynes] Poyse may mean to weight down or to balance, while maynes is an archaic term for hands (derived from the Latin *manus*). The meaning is either that Vis hoped that Nomen would bring into the balance his soldiers or hands, bribing them with generous rewards, or that his hands would be full of rewards. While the former seems to make clearer sense in the context, it does require a more precarious speculation about the precise meaning of maynes.

504] Some letters are scratched out before "reward" which seem to be a false start for that word.

Where I began, great King your humble vassaile
To seeke releife, I was my leige the Leader
Of yor most loyall hoast, the right succeder
Unto graund Opis, whome wthout remorse
Dread warrs bereft of life, & did enforce
Him to resigne his place up to my hands,
That I might be the leader of your bands.
And that I have it faithfully ꝑformed,
Se this my fatall wound, though wholie armed
My dative case is wanting, which restore
And I shalbe sound, & as I was before
To wch he answers Generall, whose name
Doth tell thy nature, & whose glorious fame
Thy worth doth ꝑallel, thy deepe-dead wound
Doth passe o^{r} weake abilities to make sound,
And soe deꝑtes. Fum: whie this was freindlie spoken,

---

506 Where I began,] This serves as an introduction to the next passage in which Vis quotes to his cohorts the speech of entreaty he delivered to King Nomen.

509 Opis] This reference is a mystery. *Opis* is the genitive case of the Latin *ops*, meaning variously, wealth, power, plenty. *Ops* was also the name of the goddess of plenty. *Opis* was the name of one of Diana's nymphs. Unfortunately, none of these is sufficient here, particularly in light of the fact all these are feminine, and the text refers to "Opis" with the masculine pronoun. One other possibility, unrelated to grammar, presents itself. *Opis* may symbolize the luxuriant prosperity enjoyed in peacetime. That grandeur must necessarily surrender itself to sheer strength and force (*Vis*) in the heat of war. There are these possibilities, but no clearcut, convincing answers.

A signe of amity, and freindshipes token.
Vis: Hyena-like he weepes at o^{r} distresse
For further mischeefe seeking noe redresse.
Fum: More Lyon-like he feircele on me gazd'e,
Soone dasht my hopes, & made me all amazd'e
ffor when I did begin, (my Leige) poore Fumus
A lack-limme souldier to bould to p̲sume thus
Tenders up to your maiestie his ditty;
That on his daungerous wounds you have pitty.
ffor though through patience ffumus doth endure all,
Yet wants he totally his number plurall.
Affect you pluralls quoth the King? affection
Bring forth effects of small or no election.
Wherefore Vile Varlett, cease of thy petition
Thinking no more of anie restitution.

523] The words "feircelie on" have been written and scratched out before "weepes." This is an interesting correction, for we see the same words, "feircelie on" below in line 525. Since they follow the word "Lyon-like" which bears some similarity to "hyena-like" in line 523, it seems safe to speculate that the scribe's eyes inadvertantly skipped two lines and began copying after "Lyon-like" instead of after "hyena-like." Anyone who has ever done any copying from another text will realize how easily this mistake is made. The fact that the scribe was working from an earlier draft seems evident.

529] Before "your" the scribe originally wrote "his m"--apparently for "his majesty." This may have been a correction of the copy-text in which the author temporarily forgot he was quoting an address to the King. The correction certainly substantiates the hypothesis that scribe in both cases was the author. See also the corrections in lines 366 and 383 above for further evidence supporting this case.

Ali: We both divers dishes had one sauce.
ffor when I put up to his grace my cause,
He askd' me who he was, whom vilest peasants
Would dare to interrupt wth their base presents
Of fond complaints. ffor know although I love yee
Non vacat exiguis rebus adesse Iovi.
Besides quoth he the case you call *vocandi*
Is very often *causa exclamandi*.
Wherefore as in our articles we declard'
ffom those that have it lost, it shall be barrd'.
Others y^{t} keepe the same we give free will
To use the same, but wth far greater skill
Soe we dismisse you, aliquis away,
And so dismist I did no longer stay.

Vis: His good successe makes him to tyrannize,
We'ele serve tooth outward & with Ironies
We'ele say, all haile to royall princelie Nomen

---

537 sauce] This word was originally spelled "sause" in the manuscript, but was scratched out and corrected to "sauce."

542 *Non . . . Iovi*] "Jupiter has no time for trifles." The Latin is directly quoted from Ovid's *Tristia*, II, 216; although the playwright probably took the line from Lily, where it is inaccurately ascribed to Salustius (sig. F5^{r}).

543 *vocandi*] The vocative case in Latin.

544 *causa exclamandi*] "Cause for crying out," which is, of course, the use of the vocative case.

552 tooth outward] In appearance only, feignedly.

Although we wish a halter were his Omen.
Ali: We'ele plot some meanes to gett him from his throne
Though with his dearest life & our deepe moane;
But pray be silent, harke, I heare a humming
Sure by the trampling some-bodie is comming.

Act 3 Sce: 2

Enter Volo, fero, dic.

Stand on yor guards what be you freinds or foes,
Yf freinds we thus salute, yf not with blowes
We intercept you. Dic: In peace freindes, foes in War,
When as great Verbū & the Nowne did tarre.
Fum: Yf you be freinds, then freindlie give us notice
Say, neede yee our helpe Gentlemen? Volo: yes so t'is.
We three dic, Volo, ffero, men at armes
Souldiers to Verbum, sharers in his harmes,
Though not halfe sharers in his good successe
As doth our dolefull misery now professe,

---

554 halter] The hangman's rope.

563 peace] This word was inserted above the line.

564 tarre] This reading is by no means certain; the initial letter is very unclear. "Tarre," meaning "vex" or "provoke," is a reasonable prospect if the sentence is read as an ellipsis: "When as great Verbū & the Nowne did [one another] tarre." Ellipses were common in Renaissance literature, for example, Shakespeare writes in Cymbeline, I.1.124, "When shall we see [one another] again?" It might be argued that "tear" is intended, though the spelling would be unconventional, even for a Renaissance writer. Even if this were the case, the same sort of ellipsis would have to be assumed. Another possibility is "iarre."

Which thing provokd' us forth from him to flie
To seeke our fortune & psperitie.
Ali: What saiest thou ffumus? heer's meate for o^{r} mowing,
Heere's corn ripened for us of an-others Sowing
Brave souldiers we doe much commend your valour,
And would not have you thinke that under colour
Of flattring freindship, though you be but strangers
That we praetend your damages or daungers
We were sometimes of note; though now through fate
The onlie obstacles of wisemens state,
We are cast downe into misfortunes prison;
A dungeon full of misery & derision.
Volo: ffortune's ffoles furtheresse hath put us together
In her blinde scrowle; as t'were birds of one feather.
To whom an equall destiny is allotted,

---

572 psperitie] The manuscript contains what appears to be a superfluous "ti" before the final syllable. The legibility is obscured, but the intention is not.

573 mowing] Reaping; the word was often pared with "sowing." "Meat" was used commonly to refer to any food.

574 an-others] The first syllable has been inserted above the word and is practically illegible--"an-" is the most likely possibility.

583-84] This is a difficult sentence. "Fortune's Fooles" has a vague reference, but probably refers to the two kings who have driven, unintentionally, the anomalies and heteroclites into an alliance, thus aiding the cause of the rebellion. "Furtheresse" is apparently a noun created for the occasion, meaning, perhaps, "further endeavors"? "Her" has no proper grammatical antecedent, but Fortune is readily understood. Renaissance English was much more lax about syntax than present-day Queen's English.

But yf you follow me that I have plotted,
In spite of fortunes teeth shall make us knowne.
We'ele goe to all the schoolemasters in towne
And there demaund our long defected ptes,
W^{ch} yf they cannot aunswere by their arts
We'ele so turmoyle them, that the Realme shall know,
That we will live in fame. Vis: we doe allowe
Thy rare inventions. heere's one (Aliquis)
Talks to some purpose, what saiest thou to this?
Ali: Why we will leave our former pposition
And onlie give consent to his petition.
Vo: What say yee gallants? doe you give consent?
Omnes: We doe. Volo: then lett's be gone, 'fore day be spent.
Exeunt omnes.

Act: 3 Sce: 3
Enter Absurdo Pedlar of Barbaria
Thus while I sing along my dittie
Each commends it to be pritty.
My wares' for currant still doe passe,
Absurd in more request no'ere was
Come Buy my trinketts great & small
ffor a little monie take them all
But now (Absurdo) cease thy pleasant tune

---

601 Barbaria] It is interesting to point out here that Tourneur used the phrase "Barbary Latin" in *The Revenger's Tragedy* (IV., ii), when referring to the grossly erroneous use of the language. "Of" has been scratched out before "Pedlar" in the manuscript.

For surelie we are iust come to the towne.
Heere must I seeke a man of worthy fame
I feare to many of you know his name
It's Mr Ignorance, his pperties
I have *ad unguem*. oh hee's very nice *Enter Mr Ignorance*
He'es complementall neat as anie Oyster,
Hush don Absurdo. bugs words, heer's a Royster.
Stand close & listen. Igno: *Proh deum atque hominū fidem*?
Its a cruell trouble not to teach *ad Idem.*

---

613 *ad unguem*] Literally, "to the nail," meaning "perfectly."

614 neat . . . Oyster] While the text seems clear, the meaning certainly is not. Tilley records no such fold expression from the times, but there is an old phrase "to stop (or choke) an oyster," meaning to put a person to silence with a retort. Perhaps Ignorance's peculiar ability is his oblivion to any attempts by Lillie and Priscian to maintain any grammatical standards. If this seems far-fetched, it may then be more instructive to recall the Chorus' remark in line 156--"We'ele be as neat, as you know who before us." Both "nice" and "complementall neat" in lines 612 and 613 imply fastidiousness of character. Mr. Ignorance's model may very likely be a well-known, but unpopular, teacher, and may be the same individual singled out for attack by the Chorus. University drama was not above such personal abuse.

615 bugs words . . . Royster] Bugswords refers to swaggering, threatening language, while a royster is one who uses such language. This line is probably best interpreted as an elliptical expression--"I hear bugswords; here's a royster."

616 *Proh* . . . *fidem*?] "By the trust in gods and men." The expression--originally from Terence--can be found in Lily, D4^{v} and G1^{r}.

617 *ad Idem*] Literally, "to the same." This expression is used frequently throughout Lily. His work contains many Latin quotations by a variety of

I thinke in conscience, all the country teachers
Doe want my methods, pish, they all are peachers
Nihil est, si ad me comparatur,
Each one comparde to me is but a prater
I aske my boyes how they decline *Creusa*,
The'ile straitway say it is declind' like *masa*.
Then I goe further, posing them in *Tibur*

---

classical authors. Lily precedes a quotation by *ad Idem* when it is by the same author as the immediately preceding quotation. This happens to be the case with the quotation in line 615. The line in Lily reads, "*Ad Idem: Proh deum atque hominū fidem*." It may be possible that Mr. Ignorance foolishly thinks *Ad Idem* to be another classical author. LIne 616 would therefore be a somewhat obscure joke, poking fun at inept teachers of Latin.

619 peachers] A peacher is an informer (a term gaining literary notoriety with Gay's *Beggar's Opera*). Mr. Ignorance is not the first to scorn the "country teachers." Erasmus refers to them as "hunger-starved and sloven in their schools" (quoted from Mallet's *History of the University of Oxford*, I, 182). But we are, of course, to recognize Mr. Ignorance in this description also.

620 *Nihil . . . comparatur*] "He is nothing, if compared to me." Mr. Ignorance roughly translates the sentence in line 620.

622 *Creusa*] This passage is filled with puns. Since "Creusa" is a feminine personal name (Creusa was Aeneas' wife), "declining Creusa" may have a meaning totally unrelated to grammar. At the same time there is the joke of the students circumventing the teacher's question--giving an answer, yet not giving it. "Masa" may very likely be the author's invention, serving to indicate the ignorance of the schoolboys.

624 *Tibur*] This was the name of an ancient town in Latium. As in line 621 above, there is a pun--"posing" being doubly interpreted as "being placed in" and "presenting a question." The students'

The'ile forthwith aunswere t'is declinde like *liber*
Had they but little more capacitie
Ild'e quicklie send them to the Uniassitie.

Abs: This is the man, his talke doth him bewray,
Well I'le to him, t'is hee that is my pray.
Good Mr Ignorance, for soe I think's your name
Please you to buy verbes tences once of fame
Cambo and *Tulo*, and fine new coynd' words,
W^{ch} you shall have as cheape, as prise afford.

Ign: Whence com'st thou fellow from Italia?

Abs: Noe Sir, not I nor yet from Gallia,
But from Barbaria. Ig: o sett downe thy wares.
Then thou has noe Italionate affaires
Wth which my kindred ever-more were troubled

---

answer again sidesteps the question, and may involve a further pun--*liber* meaning book. (For the record, the two words are not declined similarly.)

627 Uniassitie] This comical twist on "university" has a two-fold purpose--it provides a light-hearted, satiric gibe which a college audience would applaud, and it facilitates the rhyme with "capacity." There is a very possible third implication--that is, in showing Mr. Ignorance to live up to his name.

632 *Cambo*] Lily defines *Cambio*, "To exchange, and of the old wryters it is taken for to fight." (sig. H7^{v}). It seems probable that this term is intended, especially since it is paired with "Tulo" (see the note to line 428).

633 prise] Price.

634 Italia] Lines 636 to 640 below elaborate on this reference. The jokes in Renaissance England are many about the effeminate and affected Italians and Frenchmen.

Tell me the troth thine owne prise shall be doubled.
I doe not love this strange Italionating
It is a fancy past my imitating
Heere honest fellow, pray give me thy trinketts,
Heers coyne sufficient for to buy thy iunketts

Abe: Thanke you good master; ffoole & that in graine,
When they are scantie, you may goe for twaine.

Ign: Farwell good fellow. like a rare Physition
I'le of these simples make a composition
Now possum, Volo & th'irregular traine
I'le bring to fashion using little payne
The out-lawes questions I will soone resolve
Though Sphinx (there's reading) doe the same involve.
But I forgett; my Boyes have me expected,
I'le straite to them, they must not be neglected.

Exit.

Chorus.

Hist, peace my masters, this will grow to treason,
& yf it be not look't unto in season.
Did you not see? the traytors had agreed

---

643 iunketts] Sweetmeats or other delicacies.

644 in graine] Genuine, through and through.

651 Sphinx] A reference to the Sphinx's riddle, therefore a virtually impossible question.

Wth strife to make o^{r} Grammer kindgome bleed.
They sweare, they thretten, scarcelie had they spoken,
When enters Mr Ignorance, a token
Of their disturbance whom wth their defect
They have sore troubled, we must not neglect
The punishm^{t} of these out-ragious feinds.
Sitt then a while, you that be good Rules freinds,
And then Parenthesis thy selfe convert,
For I must looke unto my other ꝑ^{te}.

Act: 4 Sce: 1

Enter Oratio, Verbum, Nomen
Participiū, Lillie, Priscian.

Ora: Now I begin to feele my former riches
When concords be observd' in all o^{r} speeches,
When that the Nowne & Verbe admitt noe iarr;
In Number or in ꝑson, oh this War

---

659 kindgome] The scribe has inadvertantly transposed the "d" and "g."

665 you . . . freinds] Addressing the audience in this manner strongly suggests the intended viewers have more than a passing interest in acceptable Latin grammar--it may even hint that the audience were students of grammar (with varying degrees of devotion, of course).

671 begin to feele] The manuscript is exasperatingly unclear. If the word is, as it seems, "begin," the tail of the "g" is extremely faint. Likewise, the initial two letters of "feele" are obscure and partially blotted. This reading, however, can be justified by the meaning--Oratio is beginning to sense her loss as a result of the wars.

Hath made our kingdome suffer manie crosses,
& to my sorrow each hath borne some Losses.
ffor when each private subiect was soe bolde
To catch into his fingers what he could
I know some Nownes, wch now I will not mention,
Who have snatcht' up a double folde declension;
I could name Domus, but I'le say noe more.
As they be thus enritcht some be made poore
Aptots I know there be above a hundred,
W^{ch} from the fight indeclinable blundered,
Besides some Diptotes, wch the wars did undoe,
That now vix quatuor casus tenuere secundo.
Some Triptotes they return'd wth onlie three

---

681 Domus] In special instances, the Latin noun *domus* takes on inflections not typical of its normal fourth declension endings. Oratio is indignant over this peculiar privilege, which she interprets as giving *domus* a "double folde declension."

683-84] An *aptot* is an indeclinable noun. Lily (sig. B6^{v}-B7^{r}) calls Latin adjectives, nouns--derived from their complete Latin names, *nomen adiectivum*, while nouns in the English sense are called *nomen substantivum*. Oratio is here referring to the cardinal numbers, which in Latin are indeclinable (except for one through three and those designating the hundreds).

685-86] a *diptot* is a Latin noun with only two cases (primarily words introduced from foreign languages). The Latin expression is roughly taken from Lily (sig. B7^{r}) and may be translated freely, "scarcely four successfully retained their case." The four referred to are probably *unus*, *duo*, *tres*, and -*centi*--the only declinable cardinal numbers. It is to be admitted that exceptions arise (*mille* is declinable in the plural, and so on), but the author is not writing a Latin grammar.

[IV:1]

I thinke these losses were enough for thee.
Besides some pronounes wch doe make a shift,
To live in credditt, yet they wants their fift;
Noe lesse is yor losse Verbum, out slack
How I do pittie Dic Duc, fer, and fac.
With Volo, furo, & that maymed crue
Would not this greive one Verbū? how say you?
Long have you fought, & fearce, but gayned nothing,
Only some Thumpes & Blowes, is it not soe King?
Verb: We fought (dread Queene) to long I doe confesse,
I had some daunger, Nomen had noe lesse;
All wch redounds to the, thou had'st the smart.
But talke no more of that, lett's take up hart.
Remember't not, though bloud our battaile cost,
Lett's say whats won is won, what's lost is lost.
Yf we recount, & number them so much,
It will but greive us, y^{t} our harms are such.
Ora: Oh stay, we must consider them a little,

---

690 fift] Fifth. The reference seems to be to the fact that Latin pronouns have only four declensions, whereas the nouns have five. The singular verb "wants" accompanying a plural subject "they" is probably not an error. The form was used for "are wanting" and has the precedence of Shakespeare supporting it ("Though the bride and bridegroom wants / For to supply the places at the table," The Taming of the Shrew, III. ii).

701] After "Remember't" the word "that" has been written and scratched out. It would, of course, be superfluous, but the correction suggests another emendation of a lost copy-text by the author/scribe (see the note to line 523 above).

We should not doe amisse to build a spittle,
ffor maym'de souldiers somewhere in the citty;
To see soe manie daylie halt t'is pittie.
Nom: It is indeed, & my men they complaine,
Wishing that each then had binne outright slaine,
Rather then all their life long to lye bedrid.
Ver: T'were fit indeed there case should be consid'red,
But they ꝑsume soe much upon their merritt
As yf that from our hands they strayt would teare it.
Craving Rewards forsooth for all their wounds,
Thus still our pallace wth their clamours sounds.
Fer would have fero, but I'le fferas make
to serve his turne. some wrong he needs must take.
And Dapper Dic his Dice proudlie claimes,
In gen^{r}all for rewards tends all their aimes,
Which Ile cut of, I'le make them for to feele,
That Verbum can be angry yf he will.
Nom: You're delt wth by yor men, and I by mine,
One comes, & cries my dative case resigne,
An other saies his plurall number's wanting,
An other yoapes, his Vocative lies panting

---

717 but] The scribe initially wrote this with a capital "B" but followed it with a "t" which required him to scratch it and correct the spelling.

726 yoapes] Apparently from "yoop," a word expressing the sound of "convulsive sobbing" (OED). Although the meaning is perfectly suited to the context, the OED lists only the noun and no instance of its usage earlier than the nineteenth century. Its appearance here is evidence of a much older heritage and more grammatical flexibility.

Amongst King Verbum's campes all drencht' in bloud.
Ha, ha, ha, ha, oh it would doe you good,
To heere what musick all their yawlings makes,
Some Nownes their Genders, some their numbers lacks.
But all shall fare alike, I doe not care.
I'le give noe more then what I well can spare.
Lillie: Oh be not Tyrants, good my Lords be quiett,
Beleeve me you shall gett no honour by it.
You should change colours like Camelions,
ffancy all fancies, fearing lest rebellions
Should chaunce for to invade yo[r] peacefull kingdome.
Oh, this is not the readie way to bring downe
Your giddie subiects unadvisd' outrages:
Be rulde' by me, requite them wth stout wages,
And first speake peace, seeke soe to quell their charms,
Yf they denie it, whie then take up arms.
Prisc: Noe more of that good King, take not that counsell,
Yf wars contynewe I shall be knockt' downe still
I could endure a palt but now and then
fflung at my coxcombe by unskillfull men,

---

730 lacks] This use of "-s" in the third person plural form is documented by E. A. Abbott, A Shakespearian Grammar (see also note to line 689 above).

734 Beleeve] A second "e" seems to blotted in the first syllable.

745 palt] A blow or stroke (compare "pelt").

But when each fellow bings me wth his wasters,
Some breake my head, at lest put by my playsters
How can I live, I prethee doest thou know?
Lill: As yf that thou't dy with a little blowe,
Besides Anomalaes & Hetroclitts
May fight, yet never hurt thy head, or witts
May speake false latine, thou committest noe sinne,
And yf thou doest it but ꝑ Antiptosin
Thou by that figure maist put case for case
Then doe you ill my iudgm^{t} thus to crosse.
Part: Good Sirs be freinds, from words growes blows at length,
Pray lett us loose noe more of Grammers strength
I know that these late wars enough have tri'de you
Then live in freindship, & in peace as I doe,
But whie talke I, I know yor disposition;
Thou (Lillie) can'st not disagree with Priscian,
Who loves oratio, loves him, as his life,
ffor they be in a manner man & wife.

---

747 wasters] A wooden sword or club.

748 playsters] Plasters; poultices.

754 ꝑ Antiptosin] Through Antiptosin, the grammatical use of one case for another.

763 loves him] The relative pronoun "who" seems to be omitted in this clause, which should be read "who loves him." Abbott (*A Shakespearian Grammar*, pp. 164-67) records many Elizabethan examples of omitted relatives in cases in which "the antecedent immediately precedes the verb to which the relative would be the subject." (Compare *Measure for Measure*, II, ii.: "I have a brother is condemned to die.")

Let peace & concord be amonge us. Lillie: Stay there
Good Participle, I am foes wth neyther,
I nee're was out with him, nor yet fell from her
As well appeareth in my latine Grammer.
Ora: I know thou didst not, yes thou wer'st a meane,
To bring to concord all our troubled Realme.

Act 4 Sc: 2

A noyse within crying

Vox { Persue the raskalles so hoe, follow, follow;
<u>intrat</u> { Knock downe the Traytors, Fero, Dic, & Volo.

Ora: How now, what meanes this uprore in our Court,
Vox: See, I am up unto the knees in durte,
To come to tell yor maiestie the newes,
Out-lawes there be, that doe yor Realme abuse.
I have scant breath to speake the thing at large,
W^{ch} was eare while committed to my charge.
Par: What out-lawes quoth hee, heere will be some knocks,
Say what's thy name? Vox: Oh sir my name is Vox.
Par: What out-lawes quoth hee, heere will be some knocks,
Say what's thy name? Vox: Oh sir my name is Vox.
Par: What is thine office, come a little nigher,
Vox: Mine office Sir? I am her Graces cryer.
Ora: Oh I remember him, Vox doe not feare,
But lett thy sound come to our princelie eare
Say whats the matter? out-lawes thou didst mention,

---

769 meane] Moderator.

773-74 Vox <u>intrat</u>] "Vox enters." Vox (Latin, "voice") is an appropriate nomenclature for the Court cryer.

What doe these out-lawes? do they breed dissention?
Vox: Alasse dread Sov^{r}aigne, our country swarmes
With verbes defectives, wch be up in armes
And caselesse Hetroclits, wch every day
Abuse yor subiects in the kings high-way
Some Aptots, Triptots, monaptots, & others,
Are wth Verbes anomalaes sworne brothers,
And have conspir'd to gett what ear' they need,
Or they will make your country subiects bleede.
They chaunc't to fall upon one Ignorance
Whom they have putt into soe strange a traunce
That he is allmost madd, one keepes a stirr
For his impative, then enters Fer
And sweres he will have Fere, & ptests
Hee'le fferrett all your subiects from their nests,
Where's my imperative? yf you be wise
ffind it youre best; soe is my worshippes pleasure,
Poore Ignorance he scarce hath anie leasure
To teach his pupilles. More there be some Nownes,
Which doe each day & houre this ffellow trounce.
I hope for these same traytors reformation,
Yo'ule call them all to theire examination.
Doubtlesse we will, for sure we must not suborne

---

793 Aptots, Triptots, monaptots] These are all irregularly-declined nouns, or heteroclites.

810 suborne] A second "b" in this word has been cancelled. The meaning here is to "support," "aid," or "assist."

Such raskall villaynes, wch be growne doe stubborne.
Nomen & Verbum, we do thinke it fitt
That you doe send some Herrauld wth a writt
To fetch these rebelles in. ill should we fare
If of our subiects we should have noe care.
Ver: Madame, we will. Nom: Soe stands it with our minde.
Ora: Lett then the pson straytway be assign'de.
Ver: Speake thou grave Lillie. nowne & verbe beseeches,
Which is the fittest of all ptes of Speeches
To be our Messenger to this rude people.
Lill: My iudgm^{t} maketh choyce of Participle,
My reason is, that he seemes somewhat lusty,
Besids I take him to be very trustie,
And for because he takes pte of you both
I thinke his Lordship would be very loath
ffor to seeme ptiall in this enterprise,
Eyther for Nowne or Verbe in anie wise.
Ver: Thy choyce is good, but say, how lik'st thou of it
Don Participle t'will be for thy pfitt.
Par: I sweare by all my psons, genders, cases,
The Participle willinglie embraces
The office, wch you have committed to him
And will pforme it, yf it should undo him
This arme, wch for you goods is allwaies readie,

---

818 beseeches] See the notes to lines 690 and 730 above for the use of "-s" in third-person plural verbs.

Shall take those traytors, wch are growne so headie,
I'le be as true in this same deeds pforming
As steele it selfe, I care not for their storming.

Nom: Why that was spoake like Hector that stout Phrygiā,
But heare me, thou shallt' carry with thee Priscian,
You may consult with him, he may doe good,
And bring the traytors in, & shed no Bloud.

Pris: Spare me my Lords, for I can give no counsell
ffirst will I runne my head ageinst the groundsell.
Ear' I'le to wars ageine, you know with parting
I burst my head soe, 't hath not yet left smarting.

Par: Then I & Vox alone will travaile, come on,
We'ele to your pallace all these traytors summon.

Exeunt Part. et Vox.

Ora: Thus shall we bring our Realme to peace at last
When all those same defectives be laid fast.

Act 4 Sce: 3

Robinson knockes at dore.

Priscian who knocks, see that none enters in,
What ear'e he be, unlesse he be our kin.

---

843 groundsell] A "groundsell" is both a material foundation (of wood) upon which a building is constructed, and an underlying principle on which an idea or philosophy is built. The word readily functions in both capacities here, with perhaps a special emphasis on the decaying pedagogy of Priscian--a major "theme" of the play.

852 Robinson] See the introduction for a discussion of this mysterious character.

[IV:3]

Pris: Goes to the dore to aske
whose there then returnes.
I know not what he is, what shall be done
He saies his name is Robin Robinson.
Ora: Lett him draw neere, oh you are welcome Sir,
What have you harde of this late wicked stir?
Robin: What meane you 'mong the maymed Verbes & nownes?
Ora: The very same; they trouble all our townes
And villages about our grammer-Land,
No place is free, whereof we have commaund.
Rob: I heard of it, & you are she I sought for,
You are the very Queene that I tooke thought for
ffor in good sooth when first I har'de this rumore,
I was affeard that this would trouble you more,
Then the late discord, wherfore being ever
Readie to healpe you wth my best endeavour,
I thought for to present to you my service,
But now I see my hay comes after Harvesse,
Heer's healpe enough your number is compleate
Nom: Nay good sir stay, for you shall take your seate

860] Before "harde" (that is, "heard") a word is scratched out which appears to be "late." The word was repositioned in the sentence and may suggest an authorial revision, or simply the scribe's miscopying.

869] The word "readie" was originally written before "ever" and then apparently transferred to the next line, perhaps for metrical purposes. As so many other manuscript changes, this one suggests the authorial hand.

[IV:3]

Ora: Sitt heere, pray be not coy, for will yee, nill ye,
Your place shall be next unto Mr Lillie.
Rob: We thanke your highnesse. Ora: Come leave of these thanks
Let us now studie, to suppresse these prankes.
ffirst when our Messenger hath brought them in,
Lillie shall wth th'anomalaes begin.
Them shall he bring into some rule & order,
W^{ch} being done, we'ele cause that our Recorder
Shall come, & read the Hetroclites citation,
Of all wch you shall have the domination.
What say you kings wch governe this dominion?
Nom: I think if fitt. Verb: and soe is mine opinion.
Pris: Noe lesse doe I. Ora: Why then lead on my freinds,
Unto our Pallace, thus our counsell endes.

Chorus.

Fy heere's a doe to end this scurvie quarrell,
I scarce have time enough to change my 'parrell
betweene each p̱te. I hope this wilbe mended,
You see the kinges have promised they will end it
ffor while these out-lawes makes a shew of Braverie,
Vox certifies the counsell of their knavery.
Both kings have chose theire man to bring in Rule

887] After "then" in the manuscript two words, which almost certainly were "our Counsell," have been scratched out, and "lead on" substituted above them. Since the blotted words appear in the following line, it seems reasonable to suspect that the change represents an authorial revision of the text.

Those out-lawes & to make them fitt for schoole;
Lilly & Robinson they whet their witts
To curbe thanomalaes & Hetroclitts,
Onlie remains the sentence for their doomes,
Till which be done be pleas'd to keepe your roomes.
But soft parenthesis thou are expected,
The Participle must not be neglected.
Beside the Epiloug doth now draw on
Which is my charge, & must be thought upon.

Act 5 Sce: 1

Enter Volo, fero, dic, vis
Fum, and aliquis wth Mr Ignorance.

Fum: Good S^{r}, your boyes had need of more direction,
They cannot aunswere us for our defection.
Ign: What say you? can they not? *oh stirpem invisam*,
ffor this their negligence see how I'le trice 'm,
I will uncrosse them, *sursum* and *deorsum*
ffrom high to low they all shall goe to horsum.
Volo: Nay be not S^{r} so mover, as to breech them
ffor they will learne heereafter, as you teach them.

---

911 *oh stirpem invisam*] "Oh, hateful generation," taken from Virgil. (Quoted in Lily, sig. D4^{v} and G1^{r}.)

912 trice] Snatch or pull out.

913 *sursum* and *deorsum*] Up and down; the terms are translated in line 913.

914 horsum] This is probably a nonsense word derived from the verb "to horse" meaning "to flog."

Ign: yea yea. I would you had binne all a mile hence
When as you put my pupilles thus to silence;
But Sirs, why doe you in such doubts involve yee?
And urge poore simple schollers to resolve yee.
Si essent inscij. had they insight in it
They would have aunswerd' quick, you should have seen it
Oh such a one was I, I was so readie
In Latine speech, in Latine onlie said I
I'le tell you what I am so good a Graecian,
I need not come to learne of doting Priscian.
Dic: Come come. we come not for to heare your preaching
Tell what we came for, or leave of your teaching.
Ali: Sood S^r in ffreindlie sort say what ye know
Tell Dic the cause why he is curted soe.
Dic: Come Dic will make you tell him. Understand yee
Modo impativo I commaund yee.
Ign: *Paucis contenti*. peace & be contended,
I'le tell you strait so how I am tormented
With these hard questions. fy on't, I had lever

---

921 *Si essent inscij*] "If they should be ignorant."

932 *Modo impativo*] "In an imperative mood." The sentence at once expresses Dic's temperament and his grammatical mode.

933 *Paucis contenti*] "Satisfied with little." (Taken from Lily, $C8^r$.)

935 lever] The comparative of "lief," thus, "more gladly."

Be dulie ffollowed wth a quartan fever.
Fer: Sir Ignorance I see your braynes do travell
About their losses, for the wch they cavill,
But as for me ye need not vex you further
My Perfect-tence was gone, I ha' got an other.
Ign: Then shortlie ye will grow to better Rule, O'.
Fer: Yes. for I had the reliques of dead Tulo.
Ig: What. What? is Tulo dead? *o durū casū.*
Doleo ex animo out of minde to rase him,
But wherefore am I in the schooles a medler?
Sure, sure I was deceaved by that Pedler.
But I will right my selfe, or it shall misse hard,
Non ego diserto Il'e not be made a dissard.
Fum: Come, Come though ffero bears his Borrow'd tence
Il'e tell thee sirra I will not goe hence
Untill thou finde me out my plurall number.

---

936 quartan fever] "Quartan" referred to a specific type of fever or ague.

937 travell] Travail; agonize.

941 O'] An apostrophe follows the "O," though its meaning is vague. That the "O" is intended is clear from the next line, for the rhyme must be with "Tulo," and, in this play, the rhyme is always met.

943 *o durū casū*] "Oh cruel fate."

944 *Doleo ex animo*] "I grieve from the soul" (or "sincerely").

948 *Non ego diserto*] "I am not eloquent." dissard] Fool; Ignorance's remorse is genuine; he is clearly not evil-minded, only incompetent to judge.

[V:1]

What fellow? doth thou thinke that I do slumber?
Ign: *Monstrū horrendū*. What your smoake did choke ye.
'Twill choake us first, woo't they might never stirr mor
That thus torment me. Alig: harke how he does murmur
We'ele vex him worse, you know ser what the Law is
[Aliquis:]Why should I want my vocative? Igno: *quid ais?*
[Aliquis:]Why should I want my vocative? Ign: *Vae misero*
I would heere were sage Solon, or sweet Cicero
Or maior Cato, or some Maior in scarlett,
To pacifie this rude Unrulie Varlett.
Ali: What heare ye not? faith weele shake up your spiritts
Must we not be regarded for our merritts?

---

953 *Monstrū Horrendū*] "Dreadful monster." This very epithet may be found in Lily's *Brevissima Institutio*, sig. G7^{r}. The reference to smoke recalls the literal meaning of *fumus*.

957 *quid ais?*] "What are you saying?"

957 [Aliquis:]] This speech heading and the identical one in line 957 do not appear in the manuscript, but it seems evident that Aliquis is intended to speak these lines. Aliquis is the most likely candidate to inquire about his vocative and his response in lines 961-66 implies that it is he to whom Ignorance is speaking in lines 957-60.

958 *Vae misero*] "Alas, to the poore fellow"; a common Latin expression of pity.

959] "Maior Cato" refers to the Elder Cato (or perhaps Cicero's work, *Maior Cato, seu De Senectute*--"Of Old Age"--a work which every English schoolboy of the seventeenth century would have known). The "Maior in scarlett" is probably a reference to the university professors, or elders. Scarlet was the color of the ceremonial academic robes, and there is frequent mention in English literature and history of scarlet days, when the university officials would wear their robes in procession.

We were all souldiers in these bloudie broyles,
Some hurt, & maymed, other getting ffoyles
Thus loosing limbes, & having cranies crac't.
We come for remedie for our defect.

Ig: ffaith Sirs I cannot but condole yor chance,
To seeke for remedie of Ignorance.

Ali: O Sir your pleasant words shall never tame Us.
We'ele not be aunswer'd wth an ignoramus.

Vis: Let me alittle question him for my case,
Where is my dative *quaeso magister dicas*.

Ig: Why; in the wars you were of him bereaven;
Yet *forte* sir, it may be you may have him.

Vis: May me noe maies, nor forte me no forte
As I am Vis I will hate Ile be short wee' ye
You will not speake, you long to have a clap?
Take that then, soe, take up your wisedoms cap.

Ali: Nay, though ye mocke him do him yet no wrong
Stay Mounsier, stoope not, I will put him on } *puts the*

---

973 *quaeso magister dicas*] "I pray you, teacher, please tell me."

977] The sentence means "I will have it [i.e. his dative case]. I will be short [i.e. brief] with you," with a play on short, suggesting Vis' loss of his stem. The final words, "weė'ye," are apparently contracted to one syllable, which tells us that "forte" (lines 974 and 975) is to be pronounced with two syllables. (Of course, the rhythm of the lines would demand that "forte" be pronounced in two syllables, but the rhythm in this play is much less reliable than the rhyme.)

[V:2; V:3]

Now are you fitted. Ign: o ridiculi
They vex me mock me, whether shall I fly?
} *fooles cap on ignoras head.*

Exit ignorance.

Act: 5 Sce: 2

Enter Particip. and Vox with a watch.

Vox: Now, sure, We mett the very man, we spoke of,
Those out-lawes ar not fur, their sport's new broke of.

Par: Loe heare they are, lay hold on Vis, & Volo,
Two sturdie varletts, see they scape not, so loe,
Now for the other. Vox: fumus he is vanisht'
I would all such as he were cleerelie bannisht',
Now take the rest, & bind them, Fer: Fero yeeldes.

Par: Heere is a coyle indeed, all grammer feildes
Doe swarme wth Hetroclites, all places cryout,
Upon their misbehaviour & rioutt
This shall be mended, you must all appeare
At your kings Pallace to be iudged there.

Exeunt omnes.

Act: 5 Sce: 3

Enter Priscian wth two supplications

O misery. thus still to be abused,

---

982 *o ridiculi*] "Oh laughable fellow"; here, an expression of self-pity.

988 fur] Far. broke of] Broke off.

994 coyle] Noisy disturbance; tumult.

995 cryout] These two words are apparently made one to emphasize the rhyme with "rioutt."

My head still knockt' my plaisters daylie loosed,
ffresh enemies still, fresh wounds, fresh buffetts given,
Alack I would I never heare had liven;
Or dealt with Nowne or Verbe, or grammer-stuffe
They strike, as yf my head were hammer-proofe
It greeves me, others should be well, & sick
But that I hope I shall have better Physick
Be comforted & cheere thy selfe (old Priscian).
Though thou bee'st sick, thou nee'r shalt want Physician,
Oratio is my frend, & manie moe,
Nay I may say I have not anie foe;
None that will hurt me, *nec foris nec domi*,
But newcome fellowes, those that do not know me.
ffor these & such enormaties ageine me
I will unto the Grammer kings complaine me
And for that purpose heere I keepe my station,
To offer them each a supplication.
I heare expect my time, but ear', or late
Suters must daunce attendance at the gate.

Act 5 Sce: 4

Enter Verbū, Orāo, Nomen Robins. & Lillie.

1014 *nec . . . domi*] Literally, "neither abroad nor home," but the expression carries the added meaning of "neither in war nor peace." (In time of war, the soldiers would be abroad, in peace, at home.) It was a familiar Latin phrase.

1021 daunce attendance] An old expression meaning "to wait upon with assiduous attention and ready obsequiousness"; Priscian has been humbled to grovelling.

[V:4]

Ver: Now learned Lilly, since those stearne anomalaes,
Have raysed fearefull tumults, & gone from my lawes;
Breaking the civill peace throughout our kingdome
Let this be thy charge into Rule to bring 'm,
Make status, such as may restrayne them dulie;
Ill fares the Realme, where subiects be unrulie.
Nom: ffor Hetroclits to Robinson I graunt,
The like commission for theire restraint.
Lilly: Both shall be done, but see heer's Priscan,
It seemes he comes wth some petitian.
Ora: Welcome good freind how does thy scalp of late?
Pris: Thus it fall's out, some enemies waylay me,
Such enemies as I know not nor they me.
No: Hold the thy papers Priscian, our meeting
Hath bine thought fitt of for a generall sitting,
In iudgm^{t} of some vagabounds; thy writing
Will serve for evidence in their inditing.
Ver: But my Anomalaes, are become so rough,
The'ile plead not guilty, though we have good proofe.
Say, they be stubborne, how shall we constraine them;
Lillie: Some Verbes depondents heare do lay ageine them,
I have their deposition reddie written,
Which shall be read anon, when you have sitten.
Rob: And heere ar articles for the Hetroclites.

1037 Priscan] The last syllable is misspelled in the manuscript.

[V:4]

No: T'is well, we'ele tame those hawtie neophytes
And bring them unto Rule & due submission
Having both article, & deposition
But see, heer's Participle or I mistake him,
With that unrulie crue that hee hath taken.

Ver: Then lett us sitt in iudgm^{t} as be seeme us,
Come faire Oratio, take thy place betweene us.

Enter Participle, Vox, wth the anomal.
and hetro. after all be sett Rob. as
clarke (wth Lillie) thus beginnes.

Rob: Cryer make an oyes ˙3˙ All manner of ꝑsons singular
or plurall wch ow suit, or have binne bound over to
the Court of the 2 mightie potentates Nomen & Verbū
make your ꝑsonall apꝑance ev^{r}y one as hee's called,
upon payne & ꝑell that will fall there on.

Lillie: You ar not ignorant (United freinds
To grammers civill orders) to what ends
These mighty princes cause our meeting heere
Dayning themselves in person to appeare.
ffor why? Heere are presented to our sights
Lawles anomalaes, & hetroclits,

1060 the Court] The manuscript is unclear and may read "this Court."

1061 make] There has been a correction in the manuscript, apparently "may" was originally written and corrected to read "make."

Heare to be censurd for their outragis,
In which their censure we'ele not be remisse
nor on the other side will we be cruell,
Only defend o^{r} rights, so we hope you will.
Rob: We will doe all in Rule, nothing in fury,
Nor will we stand t'empannell any iury.
Cryer say after me. All you hetroclits, supant or
deficient Aptotes, monaptots, diptots, & triptots
stand forth, & heare ye Articles layd ageinst you.
No: How comes it so few Hetroclits appeare?
Say Participiū. Par: they are fled for feare.
But yet I hope they shall be tane at leasure.
Yea, & we'ele make them all attend our pleasure,
But where is ffumus? Sir he 'scaped me,

1069 outragis] Outrages. The spelling is apparently meant to cement the rhyme with "remisse."

1075 supant] A superant would be a noun with more than the usual number of inflected forms, as a deficient possesses fewer than usual inflected forms.

1079] The letters "th" are crossed out after "Participium," which suggests that the scribe nearly forgot to write in the speech-heading "Par." In line 1082 below, such a speech-heading was omitted. It is this sort of evidence which supports the deduction that the scribe was working from a very rough draft and that he was probably the author, who alone would have had the knowledge to make many of the corrections in the manuscript.

1086 Sir . . . me] These words, at least, should be properly assigned to Participium, but the speech-heading has been inadvertently omitted by the scribe. Since it is unlikely that two speech-headings in a row would have been overlooked, it is safe to assume that line 1083 belongs also to Participium. See the note to line 1079 above for further support.

[V:4]

He'ele still be out of Rule I plainelie see.
Ro: To ꝑceed wth these Hetroclits heere ar 3 articles
framed ageinst them.

* * * * * * *

what say you guilty or not guiltie.
Vis: guiltie, but pray consider you my case.
No: Nay such as you merritt but little grace.
Ali: I guiltles am, I hear crave but my due,
ffor aliquis behaves him selfe most true.
And for the out-lawes I was not amid them
Yf anie tumults were t'was nemo did them
No: O grosse truthes! how is this aunswer'd there?
Uprores ar rayed, yet aliquis not there?
Ora: And so of nemo he complaines untrulie,

1086 The asterisks appear in the manuscript. They are used also in lines 1113 and 1116, when Lillie reads aloud Priscian's supplications. How these "speeches" were to be handled in performance is not clear, and there are no stage directions to aid us. Considering the number of tiresome recitations on uneventful grammatical intricacies that have preceded, it is difficult to understand these particular omissions.

1093 nemo] Nobody. Although the term is Latin, the scribe does not italicize it. There is only a play on the Latin meaning and no character by this name.

1096-1109] Much of the sense of this speech seems to depend upon the play on the true meaning of *nemo*--it thus becomes something of a grammarian's joke. The Latin phrase, *faelix ante obitum*, "happy before death," is apparently corrupted from Lily who quotes Horace, *dicitque beatus ante obitum nemo* ("and no man is called good before death"). Typically, in this play, the quotation is not faithfully recounted. (Lily, sig. D8^{v}.)

[V:4]

ffor of all hetroclits hee's the most rulie,
That he begat these stirs I'le not beleeve,
Hee's not in case, he wants his genetive.
Nay we may rather make him gram̄ers dearling,
in favoring him, as he doth favour learning.
The good we had of late he did p̲cure all,
He is our onlie freind, admitts no plurall
What should I speake more of his com̄endation,
He onlie 'mongst all others lives in fashion,
Keepes the ould fashion, newcomes still detesting,
And labours still in goodnes, never resting.
ffor wch I doe conclude, that nemo's hee,
That *faelix anti obitum* shall bee.

Ver: Com Priscian we doe now accept thy writing.
Thou art misusd, we'ele labour for thy righting.
Read these his supplications Lilly.

Lillie: * * * * * * *

Ver: What thou requestest heare is nought but reason
Those men we'ele bannish, & their wares we'ele sease on.

Lillie: * * * * * * *

No: Thankes gentle Priscian & in quiet rest thee,

1099 genetive] This is probably a reference to the usual practice in Latin of using the genitive case of *nullus* in place of *neminis*, which would be the proper genitive of *nemo*.

1113] See the note to line 1086. We may deduce the gist of Priscian's supplications from the responses of Verbum and Nomen.

[V:4]

We'el punish those offenders that molest thee
Lill: Cryer call the rest. Anomalaes come forth, & heare yor iudgm^{t}.
Heere are inditements, wth some depositions,
All wch in tenour doe agree wth Priscians.
guilty or not guilty?
Ver: The matters all ar palpable & cleare,
As by the former writtings doe appeare,
Now Lillie doe thou execution on them,
Of this my iudgm^{t}, wch I passe upon them;
ffirst be they shut, lest that they goe at Randū,
Within the grammer prison calld' <u>notandū</u>,
Then let them there remaine for ever maymed,
Nor gett what ear' they lost, or bouldlie claymed.
They have deserved worse, we ar not strict.
Lillie: Il'e doe according to yor grave edict
Nom: So for those Hetroclits my minde is this,
That they be prisoned for their amisse,
ffirst in regard so proudlie they disdeine us
Commit them to the dungeon cald <u>Quae gemas</u>

1123] While the manuscript indicates no answer to this question, we may safely deduce that the culprits have been brought into humble submission.

1129 <u>notandū</u>] The name of the prison is derived from the Latin verb meaning "to censure" or "to reprimand."

1137 <u>Quae gemas</u>] "Who weep" or "who groan." Outside of the obvious literal significance, no further explanation for the names of the Grammar prison and dungeon offers itself.

[V:4]

There let them lodge, hang chaines, & shackles on them,
Untill that things with six feet creep upon them,
I meane Hexameters shall be there guard.
[Het:] *Parce* good King let our complaint be heard.
No: Our iudgm^{t}s' past, & may not be wth stook,
You will be naught, though we be neere so good;
Therefore I say in vaine ye cry out parce,
Away wth them our Law affords no mercie.
Ora: Thus is the grammer goverm^{t} in peace,
Thus daungers on grave Priscians head will cease;
Thus Nowne & Verbe in quiett rest remayning
Perfects oratio, both together reigning.
Thus as we hope, & as we ever ment,

1139 that things] "that" is a relative pronoun referring to the time when the "Hetroclits" shall be imprisoned. "Untill" functions as a subordinate conjunction. The line is read more accurately if a comma is placed after "that."

1140 Hexameters] The reference is, of course, to the six-foot poetic line favored by Virgil, among others. There seems to be some recognition that the discipline required of poetry is useful grammatical training.

1142 *Parce*] "Spare us."

1149 Perfects] The meaning seems to be that oratio (that is, oratory) is brought to perfection only when grammar (ruled by the Nowne and Verbe) is ordered. The number of the verb at first glance should seem to be plural, but the author intends that it is the "state" of peace and tranquility between the noun and verb which perfects oratio. In the same line "reigning" was first spelled "raygning" and then crossed out and corrected.

[Epilogue]

Procure we peace to us, to all content.
Exeunt omnes.

Epilogus.

The sentence being past, nothing remaines
But execution; stay. heere ends our paynes
ffor our auctoritie it is so slender
That iudge we may, but punnish noe offender.
Then we would have yee know that this o^{r} story
Is true, but coverd' with an Allegorie.
ffor when we tooke in hand this toy, we ment
By the defectives freshmen to ꝑsent,
W^{ch} daylie like irregulers rebell
Ageinst us seniors, pray Sirs marke me well.
Absurd & Ignorance epitomize
Their huge great volume of ill ꝑperties
W^{ch} be soe true a pattern of that stem,
That they belong to none but fooles & them.
The nowne & verbe, Oratio, wth the rest,

1160 toy] This word suggests a completely frivolous intention for the whole play, with which judgment the audience can scarcely quibble.

1161-71] There is probably no way of determining how specific the allegory actually is, but the Epilogue makes it clear that it may be interpreted very generally.

1165-66 ill ꝑperties . . . stem] The Epilogue is still speaking in grammatical terms and is referring to the foolish characteristics ("ill properties") of the yet uneducated freshmen ("stem").

[Epilogue]

I doubt not you enterprett for the best.
Priscian may reꝑsent our misery,
W^{ch} daylie are abused as you see.
But to conclude we ꝑmised to please,
Your eies wth warres wch we in quiett peace,
Have now ꝑformed, yf it have offended,
Lend us your hands, & it shall soone be mended.

Finis.

1169 best] The seniors are implied.

1171] The antecedent of "which" may be an understood "we," inferred from the "our" in the preceding line. Such free use of relatives was not uncommon in the Renaissance. However, it may be taken to refer to Priscian's rules. The breaking of Priscian's head mentioned in the play means to commit a solecism, and the revolt against Priscian represents a decay of grammatical understanding.

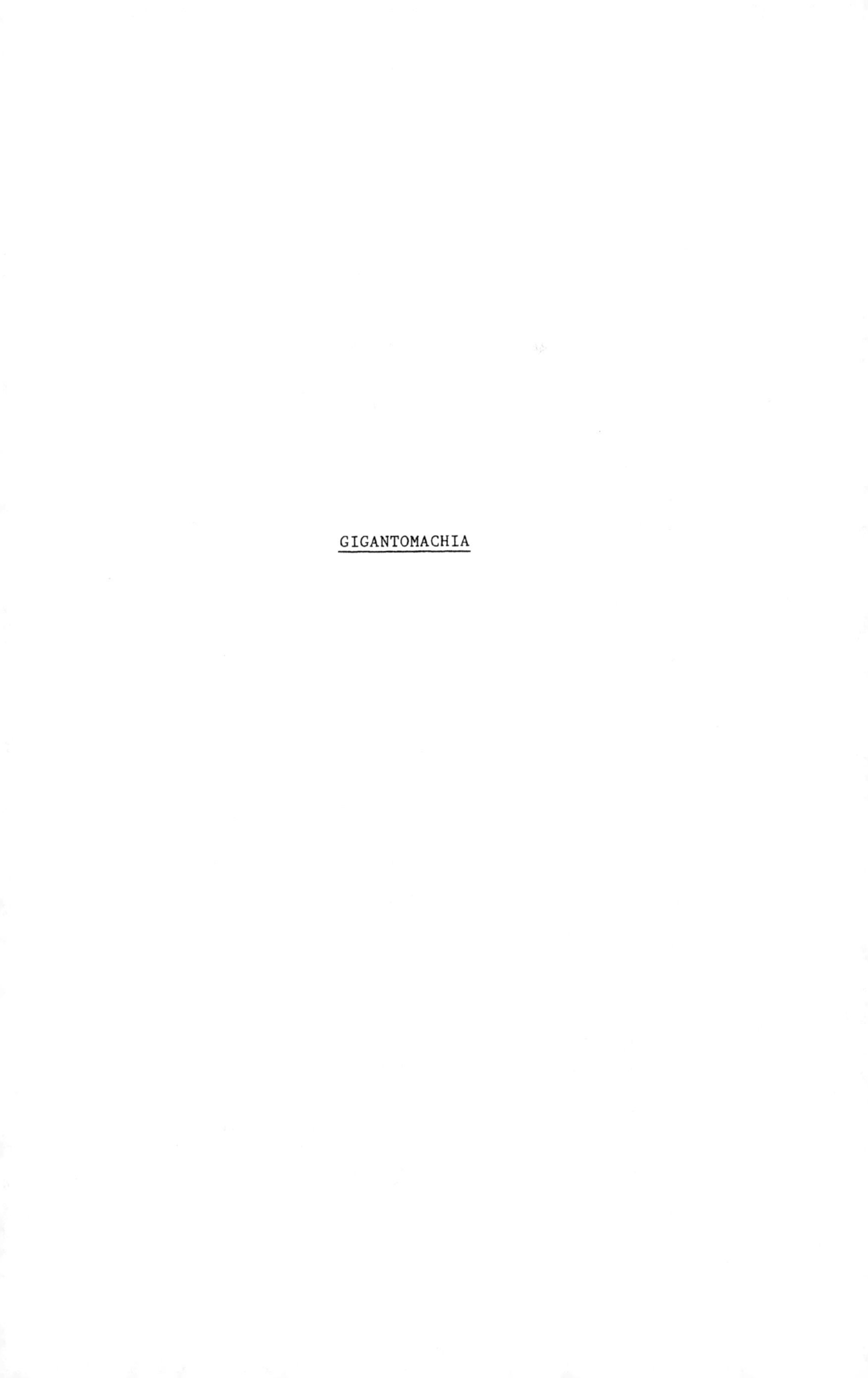

GIGANTOMACHIA

[Dramatis Personae]

Gigantomachia: Or Worke for Iupiter

Personae

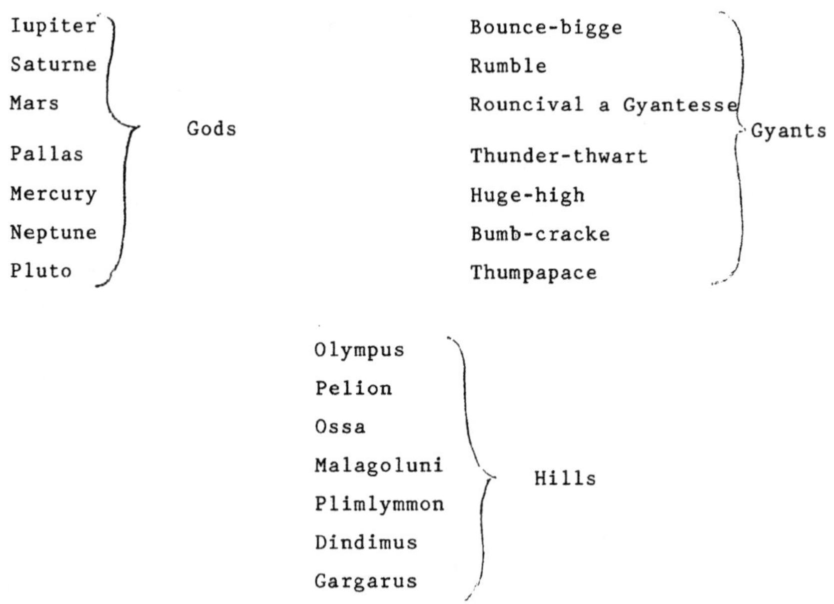

Gods: Iupiter, Saturne, Mars, Pallas, Mercury, Neptune, Pluto

Gyants: Bounce-bigge, Rumble, Rouncival a Gyantesse, Thunder-thwart, Huge-high, Bumb-cracke, Thumpapace

Hills: Olympus, Pelion, Ossa, Malagoluni, Plimlymmon, Dindimus, Gargarus

---

Hills] The only seeming justification for the hills being included in this list of characters is that players were to be costumed to represent the hills. None have speaking lines, but their personification would not be out of the question. Also, the direct addresses to the hills (lines 480 and 483) suggest they are played by actors.

[Prologue]

Chorus.

The Knave of Clubs.

What are ye sate soe close? 'tis wel done, wel done;
Yet I could wish, your cardinge still had held on;
Christmas once past, you scorne the knave of Clubs,
I am thrust out of dores, those churlish Chubs,
The boyes within there, bid me seeke my fate,
Tel me that cardes are almost out of date;
Indeed the first three knaves are, I confesse,
But I, know, I, the cheifest of the messe,
Doe purpose for to show yee one more boute,
Or two, y'fayth, ere christmas once goe out:
Yet, nor at Mawe, nor Gleebe, our play is Ruffe,

1-30] This is properly the prologue. The card game references in all the chorus parts provide a framework for the play and set a tone of levity which pervades the play. But aside from occasional plays on words ("hearts" and especially "clubs"), there is no significant elaboration in the plot along card-playing lines. For a more detailed discussion of the inferences we may draw from this opening chorus about the production itself see the introduction to this play.

6 Chubs] Rustics, simpletons, fools, but also fellows or lads when used playfully--this is the probable meaning here, and seems to be referring to the actors.

12 two] An illegible word has been scratched out in the manuscript with "two" written in above.

13 Mawe . . . Ruffe] Mawe and Ruffe were well-known card games. Mawe seems to have had a reputation as a vicious game. In one of his epigrams, Sir John Harington wrote of the game: "A game without civility or law, / An odious play, and yet in Court oft seene, / A saucy Knave, to trump both King and Queene." It

Where yee shall see the gods, and gyants cuffe,
And now, and then, a game or two at Loadam,
When that the gods at Ruffe have overthrowd 'em,
Sit still a while, and see my noble harts,
How valiantly the clubs will play theyr parts.
I will be Chorus, they'le make quicke dispatch,
Whoe ever meets with clubs, now, meets his match
Sedet.

---

was nevertheless, a favorite of James I. (See E. S. Taylor and others, The History of Playing Cards, pp. 303-07.) "Gleebe" appears from the context to have also been a card game, though I have found no reference to this game. There seems to be an obvious play on the meaning of "Ruffe" and rough.

15 Loadam] Also an old card game, frequently called losing loadum, in which the loser won the game. The reference here would seem to be to those moments in the ensuing struggle when the giants seem to be winning, though in reality are losing.

21 Sedet.] Latin for "he sits down." This direction may suggest that the Knave of Clubs never leaves the stage, but perhaps sits to one side. His visible presence throughout the play would give him the authority of a stage director and serve to break the illusion of reality (though it is doubtful that any steps would be necessary to accomplish that). The Knave emerges as the controlling figure in the final chorus before the concluding scenes, and the author clearly intends the card game metaphor to pervade the structure of the play.

[Sce. 1]

Gygantomachia

Scena Prima

Alarum. Enter with victory Iupiter, Neptune Pluto, Saturne bound and crownd, led in by Mars and Mercurie.

Iup: Thus with a powerfull arme, your force is queld
And haughty courage; you that could not welde
The weightey packe-horse burthen of a crowne,
Why, we will ease; good sirs take it downe.
Thou that to lingringe hopes meanst to reiorne us,
Weel carve now for our selves, we will Saturnus.

They Uncrowne Saturne.

Tel me with what face canst thou stand to all
That's layd agaynst thee, bloudy Canniball.
Thou on thy childrens entrayles that didst gorge,
Gnawinge theyr mangled limmes, I doe not forge
That which I now have spoake; thou knowst thy tyranny

---

32 reiorne] The manuscript is very unclear, with the letters here transcribed "io" being written so obscurely as to resemble "w." But the word rejorne carries the meaning defer or return, which makes sense in the context (and significantly, the word satisfies the rhyme).

37] According to myth, Saturn devoured his children at their births to escape the prophecy that one of them would eventually overthrow him. His wife, Rhea, deceived him at Jupiter's birth by hiding the new-born baby and feeding Saturn a rock wrapped in a blanket. Upon reaching maturity, Jupiter released his less fortunate siblings from their father's entrails and led the revolt to overthrow him.

[Sce. 1]

Doomd me to slaughter too; was ever any
The like to this once heard of vilany?
Why? 'tis a greivous sinne for one to kill any,
Mush more the plants, that sprunge from thy owne truncke,
There's none would doo't I thinke, but beeings druncke.
Thou know'st my nurses hired Taberers,
To beate theyr sheep-skinnes, as we hire Labourers,
And all to drowne my dinne, when I had cride',
Least if thou heardst me, they, and I had dide',
But, I survive, and live to recompence
Thee for these crueltеys; sirs have him hence.

Satur: O whether doe yee drag me in a garter?
What must I, must I, downe to tenebrous Tartar?
Is this the parte of sonnes? Hath your love kept tune
With nature's love, sir Iove, sir Pluto, ah Neptune!
This is your doeing Iove, an art fellonious,
Thus to depose thy hoary father Cronius;
If thou hast any sonnes, this be thy curse,
May they use thee, as thou hast me, noe worse.

Iup: Have done your groylinge, hould your toothlesse rage,

---

43 Mush] Simply a form of "much."

56 Cronius] The Greek name for Saturn.

59 groylinge] "Groyle" is an obsolete verb meaning to move or make one's way. That sense seems inappropriate here. "Growling" comes to mind, but its figurative sense of angrily grumbling appears only in the eighteenth century and later. The word "growl" itself appears but once or twice prior to that, in any sense. The old French had a word, <u>grouler</u> or <u>grouller</u>, which

We have power, (but spare to use't) this heate to 'swage.
Had nature made thee any, but our Sire,
Thou shouldst have deerely payd for't, doe ye hire?
If that ye had not, let me ne're be seene,
Had ye beene full as good, as George a greene.
Since tis as tis, we'el grant ye have a roome
Amongst the plannets; that shall be your doome.
And now y'are old, that ye may tend devotion.
Thirty longe yeares we give yea for your motion.
What powers else, unto our selfe alone,
As proper, weel reserve, away, be gone.

Exit Saturne

Now sure the world belongs unto us three,
Let's share it equally, I, thou, and hee.

---

held much the same meaning and from which was derived the very rare English "grolling," meaning rumbling. The text of this play contains several very rare usages, and this word may be a corruption of grolling. The context would support this conjecture.

60 spare to] The manuscript shows the words "will not" have been scratched out and "spare to" written in above. It could be argued that the substitution provides more pleasing sounds within the line, and the change certainly seems to be that of the author and not of one who was merely the scribe.

64 George a greene] An innocent. We may recall Robert Greene's play, *George a Green*, or *The Pinner of Wakefield*, to which this line may refer.

68] The planet Saturn's period of revolution about the sun is roughly thirty years.

70 be gone] These two words were originally written as one--"begonne"--for which the present reading was substituted.

Our selfe wil be heavens kings, because ye know,
Our power effected Saturnes overthrowe.
You of the Sea, and of all waters lord;
You of earthes netherlands. doe ye thus accord?
Amb: Wee doe. Iup: Then in, where we wil feast a largies,
That done, each one, goe thether where his charge is.
Exeunt Oēs

Scene Secunda.

Enter the gyants, Bounc-bigge, Hugehigh,
Rumble, Bumb-crack, Thunderthwart, Thump-apace.

Bounc: You doughty gyants, shall I speake unto yee,
About a matter I would breake unto yee?
If you will promise your assistinge hands,
Our powers united, whoe is hee withstands?
Bounc-bigge your Lurdane, I, though now made humble
By Saturnes brats above, acquaynt yee, Rumble,
Huge-high, Thunder-thwart, Bumbcrack, Thump-apace,

---

75 overthrowe] The scribe has inserted the second "r" above the line.

78 Amb:] Latin, "both."

82-83 gyants . . . Thump-apace] While the plot is roughly based on Hesiod's account of the Titans' revolt against the Olympian gods, these names have no mythological source. Rather, they seem purely to emphasize the giants' crudities and the play's whimsicalness.

88 Lurdane] Although the context would suggest this term to be a sign of respect, it is, in actuality, a reference to an ill-bred rascal. It probably is meant to underscore the uncouthness of the giants. (See the note to line 108 below.)

With uncouth chances, that are come to passe,
Iove that usurper, that did late unthroane
His father, Saturne, that old honest Crone,
With his tow brothers, Neptune, and Pluto, grim̄e,
His champion Mars, and more, that followe him,
As 'Pollo, Mercury, and his mankinde Pallas,
Doe use us earths sonnes, ill; playnly shall as
Appeare unto yee all, by my narrare,
Breefly without ambages or fagarey.
Huge: Out with't brave Bounce-bigg, wee are all a gog,
Till wee may heare, how to throw of this clog.
Bounceb: Knowe then, those haughty gods, are too too boysterous,
Whoe in this little plott of earth would cloyster us,
You see the earth, why, 'tis noe habitation,
To bound our valours, wee must have a nation,
Larger then this poore world is, to contayne us,

---

91 uncouth] The spelling of this word has been corrected in the manuscript, with the second "u" inserted above the final syllable.

94 tow] An obsolete form of "two," and probably not a misspelling as it might initially appear.

98 narrare] Narrare is the present infinitive of the Latin verb meaning "tell" or "recount." Bounc-bigg clearly means his telling of the story of Jupiter's recent usurpation, and he may be attempting to impress his fellow giants by his knowledge of Latin. But his linguistic abilities are grossly deficient (as his apparent misuse of Lurdane in line 88 suggests). This is another example of the vulgar, boorish qualities of the giants.

99 ambages or fagarey] Ambages are equivocations; fagary means simply vagary or obscurity.

The which if you'l consent to, we may gayne thus.
Huge: Thus penning of us up, soe stomach I,
They'l force us to a gygantomachy.
Counc: You'r right. I meane to bandy wth the gods,
Though may thinke perhaps, there is greate ods
Twixt us and them, yet since they beare us grudge,
There's noe one heere but scornes to be theyr dredge.
Why, whoe is hee amongst us, not as good,
As any of them all? I'le spend by bloud,
Before i'le beare this rogish slavery,
Goe too, you doe not spie theyr Knavery.
Though they be gods, wee be not silly men,
How say yee lads to this, what will yee then.
Consent togeather to effect this plott?
Dare ye adventure sires? Rumb: pish dare we not?
Doe yes misdoubt our resolution?
I hope we are not of that constitution,
Sit fast proud Iove you'r best, and Iuno Ioane,
ffor Rouncivall and I, bespeake your throne.

---

109 gygantomachy] Literally, the fight or warfare of the giants. Other university plays deriving their titles from this Greek root include *Pathomachia* and Christopher Wren, Sr.'s *Physiponomachia*.

121 Rumb:] The scribe initially forgot this speech heading and inserted it above the line.

124 Iuno Ioane] This appellation for Jupiter's queen seems to be Rumble's invention. Joan was a name often used generically for a female rustic and the giants may be using it to denigrate Juno, or this may simply reflect their own ignorance.

Rouncivall my wife, and I her husband Rumble,
Doe meane (take't as you wil) both downe to tumble.
Thump: By right of conquest, wee may all depose,
Soe Mercoury, Iove's heire, we'el wipe your nose.
Tut, never tel us of your Caduceus,
Light nimble-heeles, wee'l fetch our Briareus,
Wth's'hundred hands, to clog your hands, and feete,
Though Iupiter looke on, thus I thinke meete.
Thund: This hand shall plucke up Pelion, and Ossa,
And throw them to Olympus, as wee tosse a
Light tennis ball, wee'l front them in the spheares,
And each man pluck a god downe by the eares.
Bumb: Though I speake little I'le not be a Cipher,
'Tis not a petty gods stroake, that I'le flie for,
Wee will opppse our selfe in ful careere,
Agaynst the strongest, and I care not where,
And though I say't my selfe, I'le cope a loane,
With Iove himselfe, wert in the burninge Zone.

129-32] Mercury was Jupiter's son, but classical mythology never mentions him as Jupiter's heir. The Caduceus was his heraldic staff, and as the gods' messenger he was always depicted with winged sandals, thus "nimble-heeles." Briareus was one of the hundred-armed giants, but Hesiod records that he sided with the Olympian Gods against the Titans.

142 cope a loane] Come to blows alone.

143 burninge Zone] The torrid zone, the land between the tropics.

Bid them defiance. Bounc: Gods beware your croopers
Weel have y^t greene cheese tosted for our suppers.
Huge: Tis not your proud lookes, that canne turne and winde us,
But yee shall knowe, yee come an are behinde us.
Exeunt $\overline{\text{ces}}$

Scena Tirtia.

Enter Mars, Pallas, Mercury, Iupiter

Iup: Ye champions Mars, and Pallas of our kingdome,
I am t'acquaynt yee lately with a thinge done,
Since Saturne yett y^e crowne, which now divided,

---

144 croopers] Cruppers, but buttocks.

145] This line is something of a mystery. In the sixteenth and seventeenth centuries (as occasionally today) the joke was current that rustics and fools believed the moon to be made of green cheese. The line may be an obscured reference to the boorishness and ignorance of the giants, as presumably the moon would be within their domain should they win their struggle. (The _OED_ cites a 1611 source: "[Wee say of such an Idiot] hee thinkes the Moone is made of greene cheese.") Compare lines 88 and 117 for further examples of the giants' boorish qualities.

145 y^t] Originally another word, also beginning with "y," was written here. The letters, except for the initial "y," have been scratched out and the superscript "t" substituted. The blotted letters are illegible, making it nearly impossible to speculate about the exact nature of the change, although it was clearly a substantive one, and is further evidence that the manuscript is the author's hand. (See the note to line 60 above and the introduction to this play for supporting material.)

152 t'acquaynt] This was initially written "to acquaynt," then the scribe scratched the "o" and contracted the word, obviously to maintain the meter. There appear to be two apostrophes side by side, a probable slip by the scribe. A similar slip appears in line 146, where the "e" in "y^e" was altered to a superscript.

Is by our selfe, and by our brothers guided,
In our three regions, which by portions even,
Are sea, and hel, for them, and for me heaven,
With the adiacent, and contiguous earth,
A portion more then theyrs, by right of birth.
Neptune his subiects, they observe his lore,
And bound themselves in bankes, for runninge ore,
And when his herauld, the blew-mantled Triton,
Gives but his summons once, they all runne right on
The wayes of love and duty, as say authors,
To gratifie or grace theyr kinge of waters.
My brother Pluto hath a greater charge,
His teritories beeinge soe darke, soe large,
Yet for ought I heare, Cerberus and Charon
Order his goblins soe, that never dare one,
Amongst them all at's government repine,
Or studie to depose him, as doe mine.
Pallas & Mars startle.
Tis too true Pallas, and thou noble Mars,
I am opposed by the universe,
That wer't not for your peace, (except my wife)
Iove would bee quickly weary of his life.
Mars: Ambitious varletts doe they seeke our kingdome?
Cannot the earth contayne them? I wil bringe downe

---

159 lore] The meaning here is command.

164 or] This word has been substituted for "and" which was scratched out, but the logic behind the change is difficult to explain.

Theyr lofty stomachs, I am past all patience
If that I come, I'le bringe them that shall chase ye hence.
Vulcan my armour, fury bringe my horse,
Employment's toward, now heere's works for Mars.

Pall: Pray take me with you, never goe alone a,
I'le be noe longer Pallas, but Bellona.

Mer: Heavens herauld Hermes doth his service tender,
To stop this mischeife, least it more should gender.

Iup: Hour loves, our thankes; but doe ye knowe the brood.
Of these insultinge rebels? it were good
I did acquaynt you. They are sonnes a' hundred,
The snake-foot sonnes of earth, I heard 'um numbred
How mov'd', how hartned to this fowle attempt,
I know not, I, unlesse uppon contempt.
W^{ch} if your power can ought, or ought can I,
Were they myne owne sonnes they should deerly buy,
I sweare. Pall: O doe not. Iup: But I will by gis.

Pall: That's not the oath, that I did feare I wisse.

---

182 Bellona] The Roman goddess of war. She was a deity in her own right and not identified with Pallas Athene, but the play takes many liberties with classical mythology. (Pallas, for example, should rightfully be called Minerva, her Roman name, here, to be consistent with the other Roman appellations.)

189 to] This word has been inserted, apparently after having been forgotten by the scribe.

193 by gis] An exclamation; it is a corruption of "by Jesus."

194 wisse] know; the expression "I wisse" is apparently simply an expletive here.

Iup: Persist they, I stand bound with wrathfull spleene,
And fiery indignation, sharpned keene
Wth whetstone of revenge, never to slake
My angers fury, till the earth I make
An unfrequented desert, and the brood
Of earthlings all doe perish with a flood.
By stix I sweare, that dreadful hellisfont,
And that oath's deepe enough or else the dwells on't.
Amongst them all, there shall not one rascalion
Survive, but honest Pirrah and Deucalion.

Pal: They are but rightly serv'd, on iust condition
Wth water for to quench theyr hot ambition.

Iup: Goe Mercury, and both our brothers summon,
In our name will them, bravely for to come on,
Wth all theyr kind subsidiary forces,
Munition, victuals, armour, men, and horses.

Mer: I goe; and haveinge greate Iove for my warrant,
I shall not spare to doe the rebels arrant.

Exit Mer.

198-204] This prophecy is, of course, fulfilled in classical lore.

206 quench] Originally "purge" was written, but scratched out so that "quench" could be substituted. Certainly "quench" more satisfactorily maintains the metaphor, and the change suggests the authorial hand.

212 doe] Apparently in the sense of ruin or undo.

Mars: I could desire the hecatombe of these,
Were only sacrific'd, they feirce wrath to 'pease.
Pall: Forbeare to motion't, his oath's inviolable,
To make him breake it, you nor I are able.
Exeunt oes.

Chorus

ffor all this while the cards have beene a shufflinge,
By this time they are dealt, now comes the scufflinge
Clubs are turnd trumps, the gyants have the ace on't.
Yet shall they loose, for all they sett a face on't.
ffor though the gods have ne'ere a club in hand,
They'l winne the game, as yee shall understand.
Yet when Iove's wrath doth on the gyants light,
I'm sure, you'l deale wel wth the clubs this night.
Sedet.

---

214 hecatombe] A hecatomb was an offering which in ancient Greece consisted of one hundred slaughtered animals.

222-23] The Chorus returns us to the card game metaphor. There is, of course, a play on the word "clubs"--they are the weapons of brute force as well as the trump cards in this game. The game of Ruff (also known as Ruff and Honours or Trump) is the card game, the Chorus has told us (line 13), which is being played. In that game, any card of the trump suit outranks even the highest card of all other suits. The giants have the most powerful card--the trump ace--perhaps symbolizing their advantage in making the first move. But line 216 suggests their efforts are futile, for they shall lose even though they follow their first play with a face card--the cards ranking next after the ace. We are kept in suspense wondering how the gods may yet win without even a trump card, and we must continue watching the play for the answer.

Scena Quarta.

Enter Bounce-bigge, Huge-high, Rumble,
Thunderthwart, Bumbcrack, Thumpapace,
Gyants.

Bounc: Come, Enter, Peace is not a trade to thrive at,
Rowse up your clubs. Huge: Soft let's a while be private,
ffor many dayngers rashly have begunne of warrs,
The safest way is to assault them unawares.
They Consult

Scene Quinta.

Iupiter, Mars, and Pallas, aloft.

Iup: Yee knowe right well yee powers, the sonnes of Tytan
Make head agaynst us, and they sweare, they'l fight on
These loftly battlements, till they pull us downe
ffrom our seate royall heaven, and our crowne,
Impale the temples of theyr cursed head,

---

232 Gyants] This term seems to be used simply to identify the characters just named, and not to suggest a host.

234 clubs] Here we are to be reminded of the card game metaphor.

239 aloft] Clearly an upper stage or balcony is intended. A college hall would not normally be equipped for such staging and this raises the question of provenance. But the play's frivolous nature, mythological subject, and the fact that it is definitely a Christmas production point to the universities. If it is a college play, we may deduce that academic plays were adopting the staging practices of the popular London theater--and that is quite probable. See the introduction for a further discussion of the problem.

[Sce. 5]

And each uppon our conquered helmetts tread;
Let us consult, since there is such occasion,
How to withstand the gyants hot invasion.
Mars: Is not our angry looke enough to terrifie
Those meacocks? I will put them in such feare, if I
Come to them once, that they shall aske us pardon,
Uppon theyr knees, the like was never heard on.
Never was kingly lion bearded soe, by ants,
And wilt thou thus be brand by silly giants
Revenge it Iove. Pal: And let them perish all.
Iup: If they persist, assure yee, they shall fall.

Surgunt Gygantes
a concilio

Bounc: I have't, lead on, my head hath hatch't a stratagem
Shall make the gods, say mortalls once have matched um.

They Whisper againe.

Thump: I must be soe of force, now let's beginne
To start them from theyr holes. whop. whos within?
Why Saturne, Iupiter, Mars, Pallas, Mercury,

---

249 meacocks] Weaklings, effeminates.

252 bearded] Affronted, thwarted.

256-57] Latin, "The Giants emerge from counsel."

262 whop] The interjection, whoop.

263 Saturne] The mention of Saturn here is unexplainable. It is probably an oversight of the author's, though a very inept one--had he forgotten in five short scenes that Saturn was overthrown and imprisoned by the other gods and therefore a very unlikely candidate for one of their allies?

Come forth from out the holes wherein you lurke or I
Will so bethrume yee. vayne tis to resist,
For wee will fetch yee downe, and this same fist,
Shall like a massy club, light on your sculls,
And dinge yee downe, whose hee that disanulls
What wee command. Iup. That doth Olympick Iove,
That swayes the heavens, and at whose nod doth move
Theyr weightey frame, borne up by sturdy Atlas,
Doe peevish mortalls thinke for to out pratle us?
Pal: What tongue was that that breathed forth those menaces?
Bounc: I spake them in theyr names. Iup. Did you? are men asses
To runne uppon theyr deaths like madde folke franticke?
Your rashnes moves us, yf yee perish thanke it.
Mars: How now my masters, what are in your eyes
That thus with tauntes yee should prove t' be our furies?
Iup: If they goe forwards as they make provision,
I heere protest, for, I am noe precisian,
That if this hand doe once but sett aganst 'um
They all shall die, nothinge shall pay, theyr ransome
Thund: Alas did'st never heere, minarum strepitas,

---

265 bethrume] To thrume means to beat a person (OED).

276 moves] There is clearly an apostrophe over the "e" which I have interpreted as an accent mark indicating the syllable is to be pronounced to maintain the meter. The pronunciation would be unusual indeed, but given other peculiarities, such as the contraction in line 125, which serve metrical purposes, it should not be totally unexpected.

283 minarum strepitas] Latin, "the roar of a threat."

Is nothinge else, but asinorum crepitas,
And dost thou thinke to feare us wth a fewe,
Of bugg-beare words, and rantinge speeches? mewe!
Pall: Leave armes poore wretches, tak't frome me yee want age
To fight with us, unlesse uppon advantage.
Rumb: Then never trust me, but least you should say,
Wee tooke yee at advantage, wee'l away.
Untill such time yee canne provide your power,
Then yee shall see we'el meete ye at an houre.
How say yee sirs to this, are yee content?
Oes: Wee all agree. Thump: Grameries, then lett's on.
Bounc: Uppon advantage wee will cope with none

Exeunt Gygantes.

Iup: My ribs will burst with anger, fetch a Cooper,
ffor I shall burst except I have a hoope heere,
What? am I Iove? how then can I endure
These haughty speeches? and of men? be sure,
I'le pay them home at lenght, and they shall see,
Iove's power extends beyond mortallitie.

Exeunt Oes.

Scene Sexta.

Enter Neptune Pluto Mercury

Nept: Aboute some weightey matters; alls not well,

---

284 asinorum crepitas] Latin, "the clattering of an ass."

286 mewe] A derisive exclamation.

[Sce. 6]

What is the matter Mercury? canst tell?
Mer: Truly not I, except it bee concerninge,
The worlds o'rethrowe, there's somewhat for your learninge.
Plut: Beware Iove's foes then, if I goe to Acheron
ffor more supply, Ile bringe them that shall make ye run
Ile fetch Alecto, Tysyphon, Maegera,
Rather then fayle, but come shalls to this geere ha.
Nep: Wee'l be revendgd I sweare by this same trident
As rusty as a panne with bacon fried in't
Or wee will runne and fetch our mighty Dolphin
With other fishes that are naught but all finne.
Mer: But hee expects your presence shall wee goe?
Plu: Lead on the way weel followe though it snow.
Exeunt.

Chorus.

Some man will aske me, why I should intend

---

311 Acheron] The river of woes in the Underworld, though the term here refers to realm of Pluto generally.

313 Alecto, Tysyphon, Maegera] The names of the furies, the tomentors of the guilty.

314] The sense is "Let us go to be about this business." "Shall's" was not an uncommon usage. Compare Shakespeare: "Say, where shall's lay him?" (*Cymbeline*, IV. iii. 233) and "Shall's attend you there?" (*Winter's Tale*, I. ii. 178). Geere was often used in the sense of matter or business. "Ha" may be a corruption for here, or simply an exclamation, though its primary function is to facilitate the rhyme with Maegera.

323-30] Throughout the chorus there is the pun on club. Here too is explained what the chorus promised us in his last address--that is, how the giants could

To let them fall which use me as theyr frend,
Gyants and clubs are seldome seene asunder,
Why should I let them have the worst you'l wonder.
O sirs. I am a club, but yet the knave,
Put that, and that, togeather, and yee have
Your answere, I doe love for to speake playne I,
Hee that's a knave, will play the knave with any.
Sedet.

Scena Septima

Enter Iupiter, Mars, Pallas.

Iup: Are not wee kinge of heaven? and sole commander
Or all things in the earth? commande a stand there,
Heere weel take counsel what shall best befitt,
The daynger of these times, heere each one sitt.
You are not ignorant yee powers of this,
How the incensed giants led amisse,
By over daringe pride, are up in armes,
Knockinge at heavens gates with loud alarmes.
In vayne may mortalls seeke for helpe from me,
What expectation canne they have to see,
With sacred odours on our altars throwne,

---

lose when they held all the trump cards. The explanation depends upon another play on words--knave is the name for a scoundrel, too, and this knave appears to be one of the worst.

342-45] More plainly, Jupiter means, "Mortals cannot hope that I can help them by avenging the wrongs done to them if I cannot even avenge the wrongs done to me."

One venge theyr wrongs, that cannot wreake his owne,
Whilst wee securely snort and strike on naught,
The gyants bandy weapons at our throate.
What is your counsell in this case yee powers,
We must doe somethinge in these fewe short howers.

Scena Octava

Enter Pluto Neptune Mercury

Welcome unto us brothers, yee have heard,
How wee were well nigh pulled by the beard
By proud insultinge rebells, that defie,
The power of Iove, and his aeternitie.
And now without your ayd, I shall be brought
To narrowe exigents, our crowne beeinge sought.
Nep: What may those rebells be; are wee not Unus,
Iupiter, Pluto, and Sea-god Neptunus?
Lett us but knowe them, and if any power
Bee nigh sea's vaste wombe, it shall devoure
Those rascalls up. Plut: The like doth promise Pluto
Brother you need not feare, I'm sure you know.
What power belongs unto the stigian prince,
Rest's all at your commande, and hath e're since

---

355 aeternitie] The "n" has been inserted above the line by the scribe.

358 Unus] Latin, One.

364 stigian prince] That is, Pluto, whose realm includes the River Styx, from which the adjective Stygian is derived.

[Sce. 8]

Wee first enioyd the crowne of Erebus,
And were the master of three throated Cerebus,
Wee'l send our furies with theyr locks soe snakie,
And looke to't then, (whoe e're yee be) they'l make yee,
Repent the wrongs that yee have done our brother,
Twere better yee had medled with some other.
Iup: I make noe question, for I always finde
That yee are ever unto me thus kinde.
Palla, relate unto them whoe they be
That doe molest us, for it vereth me
To thinke uppon them. Pal: They are Titan's issue,
And sweare they will have Iove, howe're they miss you,
Unlesse his crowne Iove wil to them resigne,
They'l pull us all from heaven. Plut: This is fine.
Iup: ffirst wee wil sende our Herauld Mercury,
To summon them to parlie ere they die,
If they refuse our proferd amitie,
There's none but die's, or else I, am not I.
God Mercury, and unto every Gyant,
Say for what's past, to pardon wee are plyant,
If they will leave of this hostilitie,

---

375 vereth] An obsolete form of wear, with the meaning weary or sap the strength.

383 die's] The meaning is much clearer if the superfluous apostrophe is deleted.

385 for what's past] This originally read, "what is past," and was altered to the present reading by the scribe.

And part in peace: if not, wee have abilitie,
To make them vayle the top flags of theyr pride,
This tel them Mercury. Exit Mer.
Our power is tri'd,
Thinke not yee powers that it is feare in us,
That make's us sue for peace unto them thus;
Noe, 'tis because wee pitty theyr estate,
And would reclayme them fore it were to late,
But whoe canne helpe it, they must fall i'th'end.
That with a greater then themselves contend.
Exeunt Oes.

Scena Nona

Enter Bouncebige, Thunderthwart, Huge-high
Rumble, Bumb-crack, Thumpapace Rouncivall.

Bounc: Wee sent for you great Rouncivall, to ayde us
Agaynst the gods, because they doe upbrayd us,
That wee have ne're a woman to meet Pallas,
Now you shalt bee her, wilt you not? Rounc: Alas;
Thinke yee that Rumbles wife, doth care a figge
To fight alone with all, noe, noe, Bounce bigge
Ile with one little finger, and a thumbe take,
Three gyants, Huge-high, Thunderthwart, and Bumbcracke

---

388 vayle] A now obsolete usage meaning lower.

391 is] Originally, "was" was written, with "is" finally being substituted.

394 them] This word was inserted above the line by the scribe.

And beate them all at once. Bounc: Yet threat not Rouncivall,
Thou'lt have to much to doe at once of all
Us three to fight with, fight with her and spare not
And medle not with us. Rounc: D'yee thinke I dare not
Or doe yee thinke this arme, this brawny arme,
If it hitt right, cannot doe any harme?
Wel though I speake not, I wil warrant more,
When't come's to th' push, else I'm an arrant whore.
Bounc: It is enough, letts stay noe more love's pleasure,
Shall wee be fooles to wayte uppon his leasure?
Then wee shall make wise worke, tis time we were,
(If you will credit me) about this geere
I vowe, ere night that I will have Diana
To be my spouse, my masters, what doe yee meane? why nana
When shall's aboute it? Huge: Instantly, and Vulcan
You shall have hornes enough, looke that your scull canne
Hould out your best.-- Enter Mercury

---

410 Thou'lt] Originally, "Thou wilt," but altered to keep the meter.

420 geere] See the note to line 314.

422 nana] This is probably an exclamation, though the *OED* does not record such a word. Na was, however, in the northern dialects, no. Undoubtedly, a rhyme with "Diana" necessitated the use of this unusual term.

423 shall's] See the note to line 314.

423-25] Once again the author's mythology is vague. It was Venus, and not Diana, who was the wife of Vulcan. Of course, the giants may be dividing up the goddesses as spoils--Diana for Bouncbigge, Venus for Hugehigh.

[Sce. 9]

Thund: O are yee come at lenght,
How now, has Iupiter prepared his strenght,
What answere sends he, shall wee to the fight?
Mer: He sends these words by me, to wish each on
To fare in peace, and he on that condition
Wil pardon what is past, but if he see,
You wil not leave of this hostilitie,
And parte in peace, he will pull downe your pride.
Bounc: Gramercies Iupiter, that shall be trid'.
Rum: Tel Iupiter from us, wee'l ne're' lay downe
These armes we beare, till wee have crackt his crowne.
Soe gett yee gone, and tel him wee are comminge,
With proud defiance, though wee have noe drumminge.
Exit Mars
Huge: Come on my masters now we all must stand to't
Thump: There's not a giant, but must sett a hand to't.
Bumb: Set forwards then, yonder next night wee'l suppe,
And Iove's owne Ganimed shall fill our cuppe.
Exeunt Oes.

---

429 on] Perhaps, one, although it could be argued that "on" is completely acceptable here, either in an inversion--"to fare on"--or in an ellipsis--"to wish each to go on to fare."

438 drumminge] That is, the sound of drums to announce their coming.

443 Ganimed] Ganymede was, of course, the cup-bearer to Jupiter. The Giants fully expect to be on Mount Olympus by the next evening.

Scena Decima

Thunder.

Enter Iupiter, Mars, Pallas, Neptune,
Pluto, in armes.

Iup: Thus sware agaynst our wil, wee are constrayd,
To use these weapons, yet if they refraynd:
Now at the lenght, why wee would be content
To let them live still: Mercury was sent
To shew our minde unto them, wee shall knowe
When hee's return'd if they'l submit or noe.

Pal And heere he come's, now Mercury what newes? Enter Mer.
What say the giants? doe they yet refuse
To be in league and amitie? Mer: They doe.
And thus they bade me I should say to you;
Tel Iupiter (say they) wee'l ne'er lay downe
These armes wee beare, til wee have crackt his crowne.
That's all that they would send thee for an answere,
And they have promis't to be heere anon sir.

Nep And heere they are indeed,--
Enter Bouncebigge, Hughigh, Rumble,
Rouncivall, Thunderthwart, Bumbcracke,

---

449 constrayd] Constrained--the omission of the "n" appears to be a scribal error since the word is clearly intended to rhyme with refraynd.

461 that] The scribe has inserted this word above the line.

Thumpapace, every one wth his hill.

Bounc My masters, Come,
Tis a fowle fault that wee should want a drumme.
But tis noe matter, Bumbcracke thou and Rumble,
Doe but your heads, and tayles, togeather iumble,
And they shall heare soe hydeous alarume,
That had wee naught else, that alone would scare 'um.
Thunderthwart, thou and I, wee must not blunder.
But put our best voyce to't, t'out cracke theyr thunder.
You must lay load on Thump-apace, Hughigh, thou
Our tallest giant, and wee know, noe Cowe,
O wert thou, O, O, but three horsloaves higher,
Thou shouldst throw 'mongst them Aetna all on fier.
Come courage harts, now give the signall Rumble,
Rounc: Not hee good Bouncebigg, he, he, can but fumble,
Let Bumbcracke do't, he hath the shriller trumpet,
Then all at heaven brave gogs, up, up and thump it.

466] Ovid records that the Titans in their struggle against the Olympian gods hurled mountains, though, as in all sources recounting the primeval war, the details are scanty. Since the hills are listed with the Dramatis Personae, it seems reasonable to suspect that players may have been intended to be costumed as hills--or perhaps they followed the example of Bottom's crew and carried appropriate signs.

477 horsloaves] These are loaves of bread made as food for horses. Its use here seems to be in the manner of a rural folk expression which would further emphasize the coarseness and ill-breeding of the giants, but the expression is not recorded anywhere else.

482 gogs] An unusual form, but since it refers to the giants it may be derived from Gogmagog, the largest of the mythological British giants.

Bounc: Pelion lie thou there, whilst I gett upon thee,
Now I am well, make haste, you'l come anon yee?
Hugh: At hand, at hand, and whist I bravely rush on,
Lie still greate Ossa, thou must be my cushion.
Thund: Heere Malagoluni stand thou noble hillo,
Ossa's his cushion, thou must be my pillowe.
Bumb: Up looby, up, and now that I see him on,
Let Bumbcracke roare, on thy top plumpe Plymlimmon.
Rumb: Olympus, heere Rumble thus bestrides thee,
Wince not Olympus, cast not him that aides thee.
Thump: Come Rouncivall, we're lag, but weel' not hammer,
Wee'le chuse those hills, that lie besides the Grammer

---

486 Ossa] A mountain in Thessaly, Ossa was one of the mountains hurled by the Titans upon Olympus.

486 whist] Silent, or hushed. But there is the distinct possibility that "whilst" is the intended word; it certainly fits the meaning better.

487 Malagoluni] Ovid records that the giants piled Mt. Pelion atop Mt. Ossa in their efforts to reach the heavens. It would seem that the reference here is to that event, but no mountain named Malagoluni is evident in classical mythology.

487 hillo] The final "o" may have been intended as an exclamation. Its purpose, at any rate, is to provide a rhyme with "pillowe."

489 looby] A looby is a lazy or awkward, stupid person.

490 plumpe Plymlimmon] This may be a reference to Plemyrium, a promontory of Sicily, near Syracuse. The name of no other mountain of classical significance offers itself.

494-97] William Lily was, of course, a grammarian, not a cartographer. In his famous Latin *Grammar*, he

Heteroclits, that are in mappe of Lillie,
In that his treatise, where he is soe hillie,
Ile take dindīmus, and take thou Gargārus,
Now wee are all fitted, to't Iove, never scare us.
Iup: Stand still rebellious race, and come no nigher,
There shall not any put a foote up higher,
What madnes makes yee, that yee should affect
The regall throne of heaven? doe wee neglect
To mannage our affayres, as doth require
The seate wee now possess? that you aspire,
To sit in our tribunall, once more we'el proffer
Calme peace unto yee, if yee refuse our offer,
Henceforth with thunder armd, we wil transfixe
Those hatefull bulkes of yours, I sweare by stix.

---

includes a glossary where we find: "Dyndimus . . . The toppe of Ida, the hill by Troy" and "Gargarus . . . A very high toppe of the hill Ida" (*A Shorte Introduction of Grammar*, 1567, $H8^{v}$ and Il^{r}). Lily's was the most widely used Latin grammar in the English Renaissance, and it is not surprising that our dramatist used it as a source. Heteroclits are irregularly-declined Latin nouns. The entire reference to Lily here seems intended to underscore the giants' general lack of knowledge. They possess a profound ignorance about Lily, at any rate.

505 proffer] Here is another copying error in the manuscript--the "pr" had to be inserted by the scribe. It is well to note, however, that "offer" would also fit in this line, and the change may represent a revision in the final draft.

Bounc: Twittle come twats, nor I, nor thunderthwart heere,
Will ere give o're, til thy guttes be our garter.
Thump: Come give the onset and whilst wee doe mount heere,
Good honest Bouncebigg, give the first encounter.
Mars: Degenerate earths-sonnes, how dare ye adventure
To breake the praescript limitts of the center
To which yee were confind? was heaven alotted
To earth borne bratts? I thinke yee are besotted.
Unlike are yee unto the earth belowe,
ffrom whence yee had your beinge, yee shall knowe
Heaven's not a place for any of the brood
Of that grosse Element. Thund: Wel sir, twere good
You held your tongue on noble Olim a the clough,
They shall perceive wee come not from the plough.
Oes: Set forwards then. Bounc: Come on my lads of mettle,
There's not a god, but we'el be sure to nettle. fight

---

509 Twittle come twats] A twittle-twat is a babbler, and twittle-twattle is idle talk. Both expressions were current in the seventeenth century, although the *OED* does not record this particular variation.

514] As the sons of the earth, the giants were to be confined within the earth--far from the sight of the Olympian gods.

516 besotted] Simply, intoxicated.

521 Olim a the clough] This is a somewhat puzzling phrase. "Olim" does not provide a clear reading, but "a the clough" probably means "on the cliff" ("a" denotes position, and "clough" does occasionally carry the meaning cliff.). This opens the possibility that "Olim" is merely the author's contraction for "Olympus," and such a reading would make clear sense.

Iup: Nay then Ile send for ayde and strayte there wol come
One that will make yee shake, arise trifulcum

Enter Thunderboult

Kill Bouncbige first then take them all in order,
That were the causers of this greate disorder,
Die rogues and rascalls, now that yee are underhoult
Some stifled with the hills some with our thunderboult

Throwes downe the gyants

Leave thunderboult high thee to Vulcan Smith;
New edge and mettle to repayre thee with

---

525 wol] That is, will.

526 trifulcum] This may be a simple misspelling for trifurcum--"three-forked"--suggesting a characteristic of lightning. The *OED* cites the adjective "trifurcate" as having a scientific usage specifically describing lightning bolts when they break into three forks.

530 underhoult] To underhold means to hold as a subtenant. The meaning here seems simply to be that the giants are subject to the Olympians.

525-36] This entire passage was revised and the revision inserted into the manuscript on a separate page. Though the hand is similar, it does not appear to be the same hand. The capitals are decidedly different, tending to be more elaborate. The lower-case "g" in the insert, with two exceptions, is characterized by a bar closing the top and the absence of a loop in the tail--quite unlike "g's" in the rest of the manuscript. The spelling "Thunderboult" has been changed to "Thunderbolt," and "Iove" is spelled "Jove" for the only time in the manuscript. The general effect of the insert is to heighten the action of the scene--the only scene which contains any notable physical activity. The insert follows. "Fulmen" in the second line is the Latin for thunderbolt; "Cacofuccoes" may be a combination of *Cacus*, a mythical Italian monster, and *fuco*, meaning dye or paint. Thunderbolt thus becomes a painted monster. Iupiter is speaking:

Exit Thunderboult.
the Gyants all wounded

Bounc: Hould, hould, greate Iove, thou art able for to thwart all
Our fond proceedings, I am but a mortall,
ffor now I wel perceive, my men are all
Put to the worst, and I, that am ther generall
Have deaths wounde, my bloud beginnes to issue,
And what wee doe, you care not fort' a rish you.
Stoope Pelion, then that wast my stoute unhoulder,

Nay, since I am thus urgde', Ile' call one wul' come
Shall peps them all at once Fulmen trifulcū.
Enter Thunderbolt in a furies coate, ougly visard,
God herald of our wrath, now th' are under holt
With thy cacofucooes dispatch Thunderbolt.
Kill that same Bouncebig, kill them all pell-mell
Tumble each giant from his hill to hell.
Thunderbolt lets flie, the giants droop on the tops of their hills.
Die rogues and rascalls, our fell anger under
Some pressd' with hills, some knockd' downe wth our thunder.
Thunderbolt ha' done, hie thee to Vulcan Smith
New edge and mettaile to repaire thee with.
The giants are slaine, and carried out on the backes of the hills.
Bouncebig wounded on the top of his hill, speakes.

542 you . . . you] The meaning is clear--"you care not for it one bit" (with a superfluous "you" to assist the rhyme). The *OED* lists the expression, "to care not a rush," that *is*, to consider of no importance.

543-44] If the staging at all met the requirements of the dialogue, the production would have to have been elaborate indeed. It has already been determined

Let me come downe good Pelion, from thy shoulder,
ffor I must goe unto the sculler Charon,
Whoe churlish chuffe, will scarce agree to beare on
Over to stix, unlesse he pay a shillinge,
Thus the whole world lives only uppon pillinge.
But O I die, a boate, a boate, good ferriman,
To Pluto Hoe, farewel, I knowe there's ne'r'aman,
But wel can witnesse, not to tel a lie o'nt,
That I heere fall like a couragious Giant.

Moritur

Nep: Downe, downe insultinge rebels, on your helmes 554
Neptune triumphāt treads. Iup: And Iove or'ewhelmes
The mountaynes on you. Plut: Eearth and Bouncbig's helmet

---

that the author intended an upper stage to be employed (see the note to line 239 above). Quite likely the giants are to be speaking from there in this scene.

545 sculler] This refers, of course, to Charon's task as ferryman over the River Styx.

546 chuffe] A rustic, boor, or clown.

548 pillinge] Plungering or thieving.

554] The second "downe" was inserted by the scribe, apparently to maintain the meter. This speech is addressed to the remaining giants. Since the inserted passage (see note to lines 526-36 above) dramatizes the deaths of all the giants, we may regard this speech of Neptune's as further evidence that passage which was inserted was not the work of the author. Whoever penned the expansion of this final scene carelessly overlooked this later address by Neptune.

556 Eearth] The double "e" is probably only a scribal error.

[Epilogue]

Now they doe kisse each other, they are well mett.
Iup: Thus are wee reinvested and posest.
Of heavens seate royall, never shall wee rest,
And perfectly heavens potent kinge be crownd,
Til (as our oath requires) the world be drownd.
And purgd' from all theese miscreants, and then
We shall effect our full revendge on men.
In the meane time, brothers to you wee owe
Our love for your assistance, and wee'l showe
Heerafter how wee prise yee. To you all
Iove gives his generall thankes. Now letts in an and revel,
Since that the hills and mountaynes are layd level.
Exeunt Oes.

Epilogus

What? sit yee still sirs? what is it kinde freends
That yee expect more? for the play heere ends,
I canne assure yee. O then I suppose,
Yee doe expect some ceremonious close,
And pleasinge upshot, if't bee soe, you'l finde

561] This doomsday prophecy has mythological authority--Jupiter did destroy the world by flood. But there is no relationship between the Titans' revolt and the flood, and the latter's mention here may be a confusion by the author or simply a means of emphasizing the unquestioned power and authority of the Olympian pantheon.

570-81] The Epilogue does not return to the card game metaphor, of which so much was made in the Chorus' earlier speeches.

[Epilogue]

Your expectations frustrate, since our minde,
Was (as in all the progresse) soe to make,
A mocke-play in the end, yet for your sake
Thus much I'le say, they that Ioves' power withstand,
Humbly submitt themselves unto your hands.

ffinis.

---

578 mocke-play] This is clear evidence that the play was intended as a farce, though we hardly needed to be told that.

580 themselves] Originally "himselfe" was written, but the scribe scratched it and substituted the plural.

A CHRISTMAS MESSE

A Christmas Messe: Actus 1s: Sce: 1a: 1619

Enter Belly:

Bel: St, what's the matter? why doe yee flock soe?
yee thinke belike I'm prologue to some mockshow.
In this yee neyther wise men are, nor witches,
If yee thinke soe, beleev't yee wronge your breeches,
For I am come into this goodly hall
To find good cheare, & soe I hope I shall.
For wot yee who I am? Belly's my name
A man I'm sure this Christmas in good fame
Wer't not for mee what would your victualls doe?
Euen lye & stink, & mould, & worse to:
How many Butchers, Bakers, Grosers, all
To Belly to deuoure apace doe call.
If I but once grow queasy, all their ware,
Grows straight as cheape as 'tis at Barthelmew fare.
I'm only in request. for who not wishes,
A Belly correspondent to his dishes?
And now I hope to stuff my gorrell full
This Christmas. But this Cooke this greasy gull,
Soe vexeth my poore heart with expectation,
That I could eate him vp without compassion.
Well Ile goe call him. why doe yee looke after mee (he looks
Beleeu't I did not come for you to laugh at mee back

Exit:

Scena 2a:

Enter Trencher and Tablecloth.

Tren: Come Tablecloth, heer's such adoe I wisse,
Twere time, ifaith, you had been layde ere this.

Tab: Faire Sr, you are as briske as 'twere a wencher,
Ere dinner's done, you'l bee a greasy Trencher.

[Facsimile from Folger Ms. J.a.1.--first page of A Christmas Messe.]

[I:1]

A Christmas Messe

Actus 1^s Sce: 1^a

Enter Belly:

Bel: S't, what's the matter? why doe yee flock soe?
Yee thinke belike I'm prologue to some mockshow.
In this yee neyther wise men are, nor witches,
If yee thinke soe, beleev't yee wronge your breeches.
For I am come into this goodly hall
To find good cheare & soe I hope I shall.
For wot yee who I am? Belly's my name
A man I'm sure this Christmas in good fame--
Wer't not for mee, what would your victualls doe?
Even lye & stink, & mould, I & worse to.
How many Butchers, Bakers, Grosers, all
To Belly to devoure apace doe call.
If I but once grow queasy, all their ware
Growes straight as cheape as 'tis at Bartholmew fare.

---

4 S't] An exclamation to impose silence. It suggests the play was intended as part of some riotous holiday festivities.

8 hall] A clear indication that the play was intended for an indoor performance such as would be held at one of the colleges.

13 I] Aye.

17 Bartholmew fare] Jonson's Bartholmew Fair presents the most vivid description of this famous commercial and social festivity.

I'm only in request. for who not wishes
A Belly correspondent to his dishes?
And now I hope to stuff my gorrell full,
This Christmas. But this Cooke this greasy gull,
Soe vexeth my poore heart with expectation.
That I could eate him up without compassion.
Well Ile goe call him. why doe yee looke after mee (he lookes
Bellev't I did not come for you to laugh at mee. back)
Exit.

Scena 2^{a}

Enter Trencher and Tablecloth

Tren: Come Tablecloth, heer's such adoe I wisse,
'T were time iffaith you had been lay'de ere this.
Tab: Faire S^{r} you are as briske as 'twere a wencher,
Ere dinner's done you'l bee a greasy Trencher.
Tre: And thou foule Tablecloth, our fortune's one.
Wee shall bee in like pickle both anon.
Tab: And yet how square thou sitt'st, fie 'tis not good
When all men know th'art but a man of wood.
Tre: Nay Tablecloth, if once you goe to flouts,
Who knowes not you too bee a man of clouts?

---

20 gorrell] A "gorrell" is actually a fat-bellied person, although the word, now obsolete, does not seem to have been very precisely used. Here, it is obviously meant to imply the stomach--and probably a large one.

37 flouts] Mockery, jeering.

Tab: Yet my birth's better, I at first was faire,
Thou but a rude chip, till, they made thee square.
Tre: Alas dost bragg of that, th'art yet to seeke,
Poore foole th'are I aime to wash thee every weeke
Tab: Nay Trencher, yet for all thou hast not scapt,
'Tis better to bee washt, then to bee scrapt.
Tre: That proves my strenght, but thou poore ragg of draping
Thou art soe thin, thou canst not hold out scraping.
Tab: Thin am I? hold thy peace, yet th'art noe winner,
Ere longe thy scraping soe will make thee thinner.
Tre: Thinner then thee? fie cease these idle braggs,
Thy washing will weare thee to rags, & jags.
Tab: Yet when I'm soe, I serve for some good turne,
When thou art good for nothing but to burne.
Tre: Then thou wipst dishes, & tailes to, I doubt mee,
Whilst I give heat and comfort all about mee.
Tab: Nay but thou burnst, & soe to dust art brought
And when thou art soe, th'art just good for nought.
Tre: Nay when I'm ashes Tablecloth I'm better
For then I wash thee, still thou art my debter.
Tab: Wash mee? why then thou scru'st mee, this is brave
Here take thy wages, speake what wouldst thou have?
--But here come Bread & Salt; let's stand alofe

---

50 jags] Another word for "rags" or "tatters."

53 tailes] In the scatological sense.

59 scru'st] From "scruse," meaning "to squeeze."

Anon wee'l urge this matter to the profe.
Bee silent, whil'st wee heare thē make their braggs,
I thinke wee shall have pretty sport effaggs.

Scena 3^{a}

Enter Bread and Salt:

Salt: Bread, prythy learne thou to come after Salt.
Bre: Yes marry, soe I will when I am halt,
And cannot get before. Sa: why Bread thou know'st
That thou wast but a lumpe of past at most,
Untill I season'd thee, & brought thee in
To great mens houses & the Butlers Bin.
Bre: Masse well said. Salt, th'art very witty growne,
And yet noe marvaile to if all were knowne,
Since th'art soe cōmon made, thou can'st not chuse
But learne it in the company thou dost use.
For now thou art not only for the table,
But for another stinking, countles rabble,
I meane the Freshmen, which often tryed hath
Beene to the cost of good Sr Harry Bath.
And beeing among such witty prating fellowes
(Unless thou wer't as senceles as a Bellowes)

---

64 effaggs] A mild oath, "In faith."

79 Freshmen] The following passage castigating the freshmen fairly certainly establishes the academic provenance of the play.

80 Sr Harry Bath] Apparently a benefactor, the identity of whom has long since been lost.

In quick concerts, that passe Tarleton the piper.
Salt: Alas poore Bread thou art ten times more common
To every Freshman, I nere saw thee frō one.
Marke but a sneaking Freshman when hee comes
Biting with hungry teeth his durty thumbs
Heere for his Beaver, with what courage straight
Hee cryes a loafe, a loafe: and if hee waite
Longer than pleaseth him, hee will begin
To scould and, brave, & snatch thee from the Bin.
Noe place can hold thee frō thē, th'art not able
To save thy crūms left on the Bousers table.
If there bee any scraps of thee appearing,
Though they bee durty, & not worth the hearing,
Downe thier wide mawes 'tis tumbled' they soe love thee
Though Shoogrease butturd thee they would approve thee.
Bre: Fie Salt thou stomack broyler, blame mee not
If with thy wordes I grow outragious hot
Is't a disgrace for mee thou fretting Elfe
To bee abusd that cannot right my-selfe?
But thou o plagy Curre, when noe man moves thee,
Willt worke thy mischeife, woe to him that proves thee.

---

84 quick concerts] This may be a reference to the college entertainments known as "saltings," which the freshmen put on for the upper classmen (see the introduction). Tarleton] The celebrated Elizabethan comedian, Richard Tarlton (d. 1588).

89 Beaver] A light repast between meals.

94 Bousers] That is, "drunkards." Compare the more modern term, "boozer."

The Butler that's thy Landlord, owes thee hate,
Oft was hee sconct for spotts upon the plate.
Salt: Well bread, I scorne to take these words th'hast utturd.
Thou talk'st as nimbly now, as if th'wert butter'd
Bre: Leave pratling quicly, some body doth rush in
Salt: Tush feare not man. oh 'tis our fellow Cushion.

Scena 4[a]

Enter Cushion:

Cush: Your fellow quothe? how can you bee fellowes,
That puft our vin'ger like our Colledge bellowes?
Against th'inraged fire that's full as hot
As was at Christmas our plum porridge pott.
If thou wert well servd Salt, thou wouldst bee beaten.
And thou Bread hast deserved to bee eaten.
And Trencher cause you kept noe better square,
The scrapings of the meate shall bee thy share.

---

106 sconct] A fine (often of a tankard of ale) imposed by university undergraduates on one of their own number for breach of dining hall customs. Not only does the term cement the case for a university drama, it also suggests the university. The term, "sconce," is an Oxford expression. While there is some evidence that Cambridge used it, that cannot be established with certainty. See the introduction for a discussion of the play's provenance.

112 Cushion] A cushion was a drinking-vessel, althoughd a pillow on which to sit is more likely intended (see line 295).

113 quothe?] Apparently, "quoth ye?"

114 vin'ger] The word is used figuratively here for "sour deposition."

And Tablecloath, allthough thou feare not mee,
The Landresse fayth shall have a bout with thee.
I thinke y'are all like bells, or else like bacon,
Yee neaver will bee good till yee are taken,
And hang'd up, then perhaps you'l cry Peccavi,
Effaith I'le teach yee better to behave yee.
Doe yee not know to night that strangers must come
To make their Chrismas feast, as is their custome?
Leave, leave, and doe not stand thus thrūming capps.
The messes will bee now sent in perhaps
Then each man take his place about the table,
Tide with a bond of love, as with a Cable.

They all take their places upon the Table
then Enter King Beefe, wth Sr Vinigar, & Sr Pepp.

Actus 2^{s} Scena 1^{a}

K: Bee: Where are my Knights? where art thou Pepper to
Where good Sr Vinigar? Ambo: All about you.
K: Bee: Thus it befitts King Beefes great majesty
To walke the hall in state. Loe heere come I

---

123 bells] The reference here is most likely to that part of the hop containing the flower.

125 Peccavi] Latin, "I have sinned."

129 thrūming] The idle tapping of the fingers.

137 Ambo] Latin, "both."

Newly frō fiery Phlegeton: ah yet
I feele the anguish of the iron spitt,
That late transfixt my body, still I thinke
The greasy Cooke bathed in sweat & swinke,
Larding my broyled corpse, & others by
Pinching my sides with double cruelty.
But yet those hands that late tormented mee
Those greasy hands at last have set mee free,
And gi'n mee leave to see this goodly many.
Can yee now find in your hearts good people can yee
After my tortures yet more to abuse mee?
And mocke my hard fortune? fie yee, use mee
Not like a King, but I will prove I am one,
Allthough the greasy Boxes most mighty gāmon,
Brawne that imperious slave doth pick a quarrel
Against our highnesse; when the old foule Barrell
Is scarcely yet delivered of the burthen,

---

140 Phlegeton] The River of Fire from the Underworld of classical mythology is here used to signify the kitchen fire. This is a good example of the author's mock-heroic techniques.

143 swinke] Labor or toil.

151 fie yee,] The syntax is much clearer if the comma is moved before "yee," making that word the subject. Given the lax punctuation, it is not unlikely that this is the intended reading.

153 greasy Boxes] In which the meats are stored, specifically in this case the "Brawne," or boar's flesh. "Boxes" grammatically functions as a possessive in this sentence.

	And keene-tooth'd Mustard hanges upon the lurden.
	But now hee offer'd mee abuse i'th Kitchin.
Vin	And mee to. oh I felt my fingers itching
	At the proud slave who though not halfe soe able
	As is your selfe to furnish out a table,
	Yet would hee needs bee serv'd in first, but for it I
	will quicly exack his arm'd superiority.
Pep	Art thou not greater farre, then Brawne or Souce is?
	Sure not a greater King in all this house is.
	Or he that hath such a Queene to take his part.

Scena 2ª

Enter Que. Mincepy

	Queene Mincepy the abstract of all Cookeryss art
	Soe well belov'd that many her doe uphord
	Frō Christmas unto Easter in their Cupbord.
K: Bee:	And heere she is, how gloriously shee comes.
	Shee breaths out nothing but sweat spice & plūms
	See but how smooth & round shee's in the wast.
	Her sides begirt with walls of solid past.

---

157 lurden] "Rascal," a term of opprobrium referring to Brawne.

167-68] Scene 2 begins in the middle of Pepper's speech and in the manuscript the scene notation is written in the margin. The format has been regularized here for convenience.

170 uphord] This unusual word is obviously the result of a needed rhyme with "cupbord." But its meaning, "to hoard up," is quite clear.

Come my faire Queene, mine owne deare flesh & matter,
Would not thy bewty grace a pewter platter?
And more beseeme our stately Christmas bord
Then clownish Brawne, or Souce that hoggish Lord?
Wee'l scorne to yeald to their upstart authority
Or loose one tittle of Superiority.
This rude rebellion farre more stomack I
Then did the Gods the Gygantomachy.

Q: Min: My royall Husband, now I see th'art valiant
And from thy Fathers prowes nothing aliant.
Let not their coward threatnings us apale
What wee have might and will to thumpe the Salt.
Wee'l cleanse our hearts frō sorrow if wee can
As doth the dishclout the foule drippin pan.

Vin: Bravely resolv'd (deare Lady) for my part

---

176 mine . . . matter] King Beefe is speaking literally here, since beef is an essential ingredient of mince pie. This whole speech is a fine example of the mock-heroic style of the play.

183 Gygantomachy] The rebellion of the giants against the Olympian gods and the subject of another mock-heroic play, <u>Gygantomachia</u>, included in this edition. See the introduction for a discussion of the origin of these plays and possible relationships.

185 aliant] That is, "alien." The father of King Beefe is further described in line 343 below.

186 apale] To grow weak or faint, to enfeeble.

I doe not care (Save reverence) a -----,
But will behave my selfe as valiantly
As ere did Warwicks thrice renowned
Hee kild the Boare, & I will kill King Brawne.
Which to perf   I mine owne life will pawne.
When I have killd him, then Ile teare his jawes
The slave shall neaver scape our furious pawes.
And wth my speare Ile give him such sore hunches
That when hees dead Ile make him feele my punches.
I come with thunder Brawne, Dub; Dub, a Dub.
And if that faile, Ile kill thee with a Club.

191] While it is perfectly obvious what word is intended to complete this line, we presume Vinigar's courtly manners prevent him from uttering such a vulgarity in Queen Mincepy's presence.

192] There is no clear explanation for the lack of a rhyming line for this one. In only one other instance (line 548) is the rhyme not met, and that may be attributed to scribal error. This raises speculation that the scribe may have omitted a line here.

193 Warwicks . . . renowned] This reference is likely to the Warwick earldom which was revived for the third time in 1618 for Robert Rich. The title had earlier been held by the Beauchamp and Dudley families, respectively, and was one of the most famous titles in the history of the English nobility. Its holders were often powerful--sometimes more powerful than their sovereign. If this is the reference, it would establish a clear *terminus a quo* of 1618 for the play's composition.

195 perf] "Performe" seems to be the word. The final syllable is illegible in the manuscript, the result of ink bleeding through the paper. "Performe" is supported by the context and the dearth of words beginning with "perf." In addition, it can be reasonably deduced that four letters are blotted and that none have either stems or tails.

[II:2]

And if perhaps that should not make thee dye,
Beeware King Brawne Ile kill thee with a fly.
Pep: Sr Peeper vowes as much in's M^{rs} service,
Whilst in this microcosme one valiant nerve is
Wee scorne to take the least abuse of such a one
As that proude King, Ile give him such a touch anon
Shall make him know King Beefe hath servants stronge enough
To hold out tack with him, I and that longe enough,
Wee are full fead with solid Beefe & Mutton
Tut, tut, wee care not for King Brawne a button.
K: Bee: O most Herculean spirit Hector of Troy
Wee hee cōpar'd to thee was but a boy
And stout Achilles arm'd with rage & steele
Whose valour (as they say) lay in his heale,
Now wee'l to parly faith Brawne I'le talke wth thee,
Come sweete Queene Mincepy, will you walke wth mee.
Q: Min: With all my heart, and when the villian rayles,
I'le plucke his venemous tounge out wth my nayles.
Exeunt

---

203 fly] This was a festival observed by the cooks at Oxford. The play Narcissus, a Twelfth Night Merriment (edited by M. L. Lee, 1893) says of the cooks: "They have sett a little porch before so great an house, and have called their show the flye." The fact that this seems to have been exclusively an Oxford custom helps further to establish this play as a product of that university. See the note to line 106 above and the introduction.

209 hold out tack] That is, to endure or hold one's own.

Scena 3^{a}

Enter King Brawne, and the Lord Souce,
his sonne, Mustard, his attendant.

K: Bra: Thus from the Souce-tub where in woefull plight
I have laine bathing, come I to the light.
My deare Sonne, Souce, & thou my faithfull Mustard,
How glad I see you, oh I have beene thrust hard
In that darke dungeon, bound with hempen cord,
Rowld like a footeball, but am now restord
I have beene much abusd by gret King Beefe.
But wee will not bee trode thus under foote
Whil'st Mustard, my Sonne Souce & I stand to't.
Thou art a King, then beare a Kingly spiritt,
And set thy selfe as high as thou dost meritt.
Thou now art in the favour of the people.
As high I thinke in conscience as Paules steeple.
Then doe not let that proud King put thee downe.
Feare not those paltry hornes that guard his crowne.
Ile keepe the custome still inviolable,
Brawne shall bee brought first to the Christmas table.

Must: I marry shall hee can it not suffice him
That all the yeare men doe soe highly prize him

---

241 W. E. Mead points out in his study *The English Medieval Feast*, "The boar's head was for some reason especially esteemed, particularly at Christmas, and was brought to the table with stately ceremonial, attended by music. This custom is still maintained on Christmas Day at Queen's College, Oxford" (p. 86). Either this custom or a variation of it may be intended.

But nowe to when wee only are in season,
Hee must bee the cheife man. Tut there's noe reason.
Sou: Give him but once an inch, hee'l take an elle,
And thus 'twill bee, till wee his bowldnes quell.
Hee and his fellowes all shall know prince Souce,
When fit occasion serves, will prove noe Mouce.
Let us prepare our armies mighty Brawne.
I' shall prove the bloudiest fight that ere was sawne.
K: Bra: I thinke thou art a witch thou read'st soe right,
I promise you 't will prove a bloudy fight.
Wee'l make the welkin roare, & Phoebus hee
Shall come downe tumbling from his Appletree Axell tree
The terrour of our weapons furious clangor
Shall move great Iupiter himselfe to anger.
Thou Souce shallt bee our great Leiftenant generall
I thinke more ready for this battell then are all
A younge Porkes spearerib Souce shall bee thy speare
Our selfe our owne shield to the field will beare

246] This proverbial phrase was common through eighteenth century. (An English ell was a measurement of 45 inches.)

251 sawne] The OED does not record this precise spelling variation of the past participle of "see," but "sawen" is recorded. The context leaves little question as to what is intended.

255 Appletree Axell tree] In the manuscript, "Axell tree" is written directly beneath "Appletree" and is in the same hand. Surely, "Axell tree," the pole of heaven in mythology, is intended. "Appletree" is probably a copying mistake.

Thus arm'd wee doe not feare (& 'tis noe wonder)
Should Iove descend to fight with us in thunder
I hope thou'lt stirre thy stumps as lively Mustard
As the brave combatants at longe spoone, & Custard.

Must: Doubt not my valour noble King, our foes
Ere they see mee, shall feele mee in their nose.
And as the Mouce doth kill the Elephant, soe
I meane to kill King Beefe before I goe.
I feare not Vinigar, nor spruce Sr Pepper
Nor yet Queene Mincepy, but if I once gett her,
I'le make her Queenshipp know I am able to make
Her tumble downe into my Chrismas stomacke.

Sou: But first I thinke it fit, that wee goe finde
King Beefe out, and to know the rebells minde.
Perhapps having better thought on't, hee will yealde,
Before wee bringe our forces to the fielde.

K: Bra: Thou counsell'st well and like our princely sonne
Wee'l make some hast to have this battell done,
Least if the guests should find us in this fury
In their unmercifull jaws they should us bury.

---

279 battell] The manuscript does not permit a clear reading. There is no doubt about the word, but the vowel here transcribed as "e" is very indistinct. From the many seventeenth-century spellings of this word, the most likely has been chosen.

280-81] The fact that doom is at hand for all the Christmas foods as soon as the household guests arrive and begin eating does nothing to ease the growing hostilities.

Lett's goe to parly then, Mustard bee neere mee.
Must: Unlesse you wipe mee of, you neede not feare mee.
Exeunt omnes.

Scena 4^{a}

Bread, Salt, Trencher, & the rest
stepp forth and speake:

Salt: Now Bread you need not strive who shall bee greater,
For if this discord holds, you'l want an eater.
Brea: And thou to. Table: But mee thinkes I'm overjoyd,
By this means I am kept still unanoyd.
They will not bee made freinds in hast I hope,
Soe shall my Landresse Jane both paynes & sope.
Tren: I am of thy mind Tablecloath. Cush: I doubt
Cushion will not soe soone bee worne out.
Thus when wee feast least, then doe wee save best,
And in our propper mansions take our rest.
But let us watch a while least unawares
The Cooke should reconcile these furious jarres.
Lett's take our places: heare comes boundles Belly.
Hee smells a feast. Brea: 'St by and by hee'l tell you.
They goe to thier places againe.

Sce: 5^{a}

Enter Belly:

---

301 you] Here, and again in lines 442 and 444, this word is rhymed with the long e, suggesting that the pronunciation should be close to "ye."

[III:1]

Belly: Oh that this Beefe and Brawne were but in jest,
Soe might I sooner come unto this feast.
Since they must bee eaten both, what need they strive
Who shall bee first killd or who last alive?
The divell's in the Cooke that cannot keepe
Them in the Kitchin: sure the old knaves asleepe.
My stomach told mee some two howres agoe
'Twas supper time, but I scarce finde it soe.
They on whome I should eate (I meane the meate)
Are ready one another for to eate.
I'le waite on thē awhile, but when I light on thē
Upon the Table, oh how I will bite on them.
If I bee partiall, let mee bee hang'd up.
Tis not an oxe can conquer my vast gut?
Ile goe & whet my teeth for thy good cheere;
In the meane time beware your Christmas beere.
Exit.

Brea: I told yee soe, lett's stay and see the ende
Heere comes King Beefe.
Cush: hee lookes not like Brawnes freind

Actus 3^{a} Scena 1^{a}

Enter K. Beefe with Sr Vinigar, & Sr Pepper.

K: Bee: What say our Knights? what doe our enemies meane?
To fight it out, or to forsake us cleane?
Hast thou descride armies? if thou hast
Tell us that wee may make the greater host.

Vin: Brawnes sonne, Lord Souce, comes dropping wth him to.
Oh wee shall have a pittifull adoe.
Souce needes noe other weapon but his smell,
Twould choake one though hee were brought up in hell.
Mustard is feareles; hee contemnes his foes,
Oh sayth here, let mee have them by the nose.
Thus my dread Leige, are you on each side layde for.

K: Bee: Courage my Subjects, what are yee affraid for?
Thinke you our forces can not maister theirs?
Why what is Brawne? or what is Souce that dares
Compare his hoggish forces to our might?
Will they deny great Oxes sonne his right?
Was not my father king of all the heard?
And shall his sonne by hoggs bee made affeard?
Have wee not equall healpe? why, then, what care I
Full flesh, stiff ribbs & branches of Rosemary.

Pep: My Lord, you servant vowes to stand
In your defence as longe as heare's a hand
And though I cannot wounde with deadly wronge,
Let mee along to bite them by the tounge.

Vin: And Vinigar sweares hee will play his part,

---

331 dropping] Referring both to the juices falling off the roasting meat and to the dripping of the sauce made to serve over the meat. The term is also, of course, meant to be denigrating.

346] This is a rallying cry in a typical heroic fashion. The weapons of Rosemary branches are mentioned again in line 386.

Though hee bee not soe stronge, hee's quick & tart.
Thou Pepper shallt inflame and I will coole,
Ile make them looke as though they were at stoole.
K: Bee: Why thus it should bee, but what armes, what weapons
Shall wee advance against these fearfull Capons.
I'le beare my Fathers horne to goare the slaves,
I there's a toole will send them to their graves.
Vin: What if your fathers horne cannot bee found?
K: Bee: Are there not horned beastes enough on grownd?
Or if the fields bee scant, & can not fitt yee,
Yee may finde hornes to many in the citty.
Pep: Twas well thought on my Leige, shall wee bee packing?
And see that nothinge for the time bee lacking?
K: Bee: I come letts goe; Brawne wee'l not doubt you S^r,
Come Vinigar. Vin: Ile clinge about you S^r.

Scena 2^a

Enter King Brawne, and the Lord Souce
his sonne, Must: his attendant to thē going out

K: Bra: Stand wide, give roome, I come thou roasted slave:
What dar'st thou thus on our owne grownd to brave?
Think'st thou that 'cause I've layne a longe time cold,
And in my wet hoale was allmost growne old,
Will give my place to thee? if soe take heed.
My power is comming on: Subjects proceed.

---

354 at stoole] Another scatalogical reference (see note to line 53).

Fix't heer's my Fathers tuske to meet thy horne,
It hath destroy'd full many a good Acorne.
Then heer's his bristles thrice as tough as stickes
Shall pierce thy sides farre worse then Butchers prickes.

K: Bee: Wee feare thee not thou massy thick-skind churle.
This horne shall thee from of the table hurle,
If thou put foote beefore mee, it shall goare thee
Worse then the knife the Sire that went beefore thee.
Then heer's my rib, with this same cragged stump
Thy sencelesse souce-sok't sides Ile thwack & thumpe.
Lastly these stubbed branches of Rosemary
Shall digge your hide iffaith Sr Ile not spare you.

K: Bra: Thou overrosted slave, I feare thee not.
Take heede this crooked engine teare thee not
Were't not I for some worthy followers waite
My men & I would bid thee battell straight.
But stay till all come in thou black-burnt Beefe
Wee'l new beelard your ribbs, and to bee breife
Soe teare your bloud-dry'd gravy-swelling corse,
That hungry teeth shall rage with lesse remorse.

---

377 Acorne] Hogs were known for their diet of acorns.

383] An ellipsis, "worse than the knife gored the sire that went before thee." "Sire" may refer to King Brawne's father, or simply to the last boar butchered.

394-95] This is an attack on the sometimes unappetizing toughness of beef.

K: Beef: Well Brawne, wee'l meete i'th' shambles, 'tis not farre.
Wee'l try of what solidity you are.

Exeunt:

Manent Vin. & Mustard.

Vinig: Thou villaine, why did'st thrust mee? thinkst thou still
Wee are together in the Mustard mill?

Must: I thrust thee not thou musty sun-burnt slave,
Yet thinkest thou the wall of mee shallt have?
Proud Princkoxe know I am thy better nowe
And waite upon a worthier dish then thou.

Vin: O Traitour to my Lord King Beefe! have I
Healp't for to moyst thy seede when thou wast dry.
Have I created thee, & gi'n thee spirit,
That thou should'st strive my honour to inherit?
Ungratefull wretch, back or Ile wash thee thin
Better thou hadd'st thy woodden house beene in,
Goe learne more wit of that grave ancient pot,
That will yet tell thee if thou remembrest not
How oft I have increasd thee at the bottom
And more good turnes, allthough thou hast forgot 'em
Remember how I washt thy dreggs out once

---

396 shambles] A pun is probably intended here. The "shambles" was a meat market where the butchering was often done, but figuratively the word refers to a place of carnage and bloodshed.

403] From the old expression, "to have the wall," the position of greater respect.

406-17] This whole speech refers to the culinary fact that vinegar is the principal ingredient of mustard.

To serve i'th hall that sav'd the Cooke a sconce.
Must: Do'st thou bely that honest fellow to?
O thou soure Varlet! what willt thou not doe?
That rayl'st against soe good a freind of thine?
Have I not seene him with these eyes of mine,
When thou with butter should'st i'th'hall have gon,
For thy more credit send thee in alone?
Vin: Nay if you goe to that, how oft have I
Sav'd him, when hee hath beene at poynt to dye?
For when a loathsome rotten egge oft comes
And the soft geare runnes all about his gummes,
Did not I Vinigar aneare him stande
To wash his mouth, hee would perish out of hand.
Must: Nay that's starke false, for though thou next him bee
I could drive out the sent, as well as thee.
Vini: But thou willt put him to a double paine,
H' had neede of bread to drive thee out againe.
Must: Thou sland'rest him & mee, think'st thou his nose
Can not indure such fleabitings as those?
That usd to choaking savours, ever fighting
With the hot vapour of old Linge & Whiting.
Hee that with open nostrills lookes on these,

---

427 geare] A rather unappetizing thought, but "geare" is "pus," from the rotten egg.

428 aneare] Close by.

437 Linge & Whiting] Both are varieties of common English food fish.

May spoone mee up, and beare't away with ease.
But I'le indure noe more your scornefull taunts,
Try't with your bilbowe, let that scoule your vaunts.
Vini: You're very hot Sr Mustard, 't would beseeme you
To know my presence, howsoe'r you deeme mee.
But since you are upon the spur I'm for you
And yet mee thinkes againe I'm somewhat sorry,
Knowing thou art mine owne begotten creature.
And how I've healp'd to fabricate thy nature
That nowe I should undoe what I have done
Does somewhat move mee: yet 'twast thou beegun.
Have at your hide: alas! now in good trooth,
Say I should kill thee, I'de bee very loath,
But yet I'm urg'd; he, tell mee wilt thou yeald,
Beafore thou tryst the terrour of the field?
Must: Yeald? think'st thou I was borne to shame
The honour of the high Sinapian name?
Or give a foote of grownd to such as thee?
A poore thin rascall in respect of mee
Noe try feeble forces; I'le not spare thee,
Come thou must dy, poore Vinigar prepare thee.
Vini: Nay Mustard stay, wee'l combate in the battaile,
Letts bleed in warre, & not in peace like cattle.

---

441 bilbowe] A sword.

455 Sinapian] From the Latin, _sināpis_, "mustard." The word appears to be a coinage of the author.

Must: It shall not serve your turne, or fight or dy.
Vin: Oh stay I am not ready, too't by 'nd by:
I'le but goe whet my sword, & come agen:
Lett's have faire play, and equall ods like men.
Must: S^{r} try your blade one boute, 'tis keane enough,
Were but your selfe of answerable stuff.
Vini: Then give mee leave to take my fees, & runne,
And come upon thee like a thund'ring gunne.
Thus I retire my selfe, now thinke on hell,
Thither Ile send thee anon, till then farewell
(Hee runns away

Sce: 3^{a}

Enter Belly

Belly: Oh that this Beefe & Brawne would but have donne.
I'm sure I pine for't. I that was a tonne
In compasse, now am lesse then any ferkin:
See but how much there wantes to fill this jerkin.
Oh how my gutts within my bulke doe rumble,
Sometimes they crawle, sometimes they rowle, and tumble.
All while this Cooke, this idle Cooke goes peaking
For Beefe & Brawne in every corner sneaking
Cooke and bee hang'd make hast do'st meane to starve mee,
Send in the meate, or thou thy selfe shallt serve mee.

---

477 ferkin] A small cask for storing liquids or foods.

Ile not bee made to stand heere like a noddy,
Whil'st all my gutts runne up and downe my boddy.
Nor yet? Ile fetch thee then, your chopping knife
Shall hardly from these teeth defend your life
And yet it will, 'twere better to intreat him
Then to provoke his anger, and to threat him
Therefore I'le goe in humble manner to him,
And to take upp this quarrel I will woo him
Till I perswade him to't Ile never linne,
Soe shall I stuff this doublet growne soe thin
Exit to the Cooke.

Act 4 Sce: 1ª

Cooke: Oh who would bee a Cooke to sweat & swagger
For other men? oh that I had I dagger
I'de tame this Beefe and Brawne, & thier whole rout.
I mervaile how the Divell this Brawne gat out,
Or Beefe, when as I charg'd them goe noe farther
Then the stronge Barracadoes of my larder.
But yet they have transgresst our sterne com̄and.
They're free, but I must to the danger stand.

---

485 noddy] A simpleton, fool.

493 linne] I.e., cease, leave off.

498 oh . . . dagger] The redundant "I" in this clause is difficult to explain--"my" is expected and there is no grammatical precedent for using the subjective case here. It is either a quirk of the Cooke's speech--see line 505 below--or simply a scribal error.

And I though I stirre my stumps in what I can,
To give content to all, yet ev'ry man
Will bee upon my jacket; and the Cooke
Alone must to a world of busines looke
One hungry fellow runnes about & wishes
Hee could but finde the Cooke, I then the dishes
Should fly about--the rest of them they rave
And cry where is our meate? this Cooke's a knave.
And how alas can I provide them meate
When as that's runne away, wch they should eate.
I heare that they fall out because I ment
To serve Brawne in first but what's thier intent
After this quarrel that Ile search anon
O that I knew but whither they are gonne
I'de quicly fetch them in, & make them know
I am of some authority I trow.

Sce: 2^{a}

Enter Belly.

Belly: Now is the time for him that coggs and flatters.
Now I'le stepp forth: Great King of dishes, platters,
Foule dripping panns & spitts: sole Lord, and Master
Of that good cheere, whereof I'de faine bee taster
Great Duke of Chimnies famous territory,

---

510 I] This should be read "Aye" followed by a comma.

523 coggs] Cheats or deceives.

[IV:2]

Heare mee with patience, whil'st I tell a story.
Cooke: Oh Mr Belly S^{r} I know your minde:
I'm sure you hope good victualls heere to finde,
I would I had it for you, but to say
The truth both Beefe & Brawne are runne away.
Belly: I kno't (right well) but I can tell you
Of all thier complotts; doe you thinke that Belly
Smells not out Beefe & Brawne in ev'ry corner,
I & Queen Mincepy, though some teeth had torne her.
Cooke: O blesse mee with this news. Belly by Gis
I sweare thou shallt fare farre better for this.
Ile stuff thy greedy all devouring ponch
With delicates wch shall thy hunger stonch.
Wee'l teach thee to forget to eate butterd fish,
Some Phenix at the least shall bee thy dish.
O tell mee then but where as these extravagants,
That wee to fetch them home may have a gante.
Belly: Soe please your Sattin doublett's greasy gravity,
I'le tell you all I know and now S^{r} have at you.
Thou great Apollo, who's sweet harpe is strunge soe well,

---

537 by Gis] An exclamation ("by Jesus").

540 stonch] That is, "satisfy."

543 as] This may be a scribal error for "ar." Otherwise, the sense is unclear.

544 gante] Perhaps "gantry"--"a four-footed wooden stand for barrels" (<u>OED</u>). "Gante" is also a form for "gannet"--the Solan goose--but this reading seems unlikely.

[IV:2]

Guide mee now speaking, that cann'st rule the tounge soe
A bloudy quarrell must by mee describ'd bee
But should they come, oh tell mee where to hide mee.
Cooke: Tut feare not man, I warrant thee th'art free
They'l tremble all, when they but looke on thee.
Belly: Then know (Great S^{r}) and I may tell it you,
They'v gonne to th' field to fight, beeleav't 'tis true,
You know the reason, & 't was my intent
To tell your worshipp what these roysters meant.
But I poore I by this meanes have not din'd,
See how I'm falne away, see how I'm pin'd.
Unlesse your worshipp will vouchsafe some ayde
To mee now allmost desperate, I'm affraide,
T'will bee a meanes that I for want of meate
Shall bee my selfe made food for crowes to eate.
Cooke: Feare not my noble Belgicus, for I
Will goe & look out for them by & by.

---

548 soe] The absence of a rhyme here is difficult to explain, unless we assume that the author intended the line to conclude with "soe well." Both the alexandrine and the feminine rhyme would be in character with the playwright's style.

563 Cooke:] The scribe mistakenly wrote "Belly" for this speech heading, then carefully drew two lines through the word and substituted the correct, "Cooke," below. See the note to line 255 for a further comment on scribal corrections.

563 Belgicus] This mock-heroic appellation is probably derived from the warlike Germanic tribe, the Belgae.

Know'st thou the place? <u>Bel</u>: I doe, for I heare say
Tis at the Market, this the very day.
The houre's at hand. Coo: Then wee will goe & parte
That Beefe & Brawne, that beare's so stout a hart.
Lett's hast, mee thinkes I heare the scollers say
Where is this Cooke, this knave? hee's runne away.
Then followe mee my selfe will ende the strife
With noe small weapon, with my chopping knife.

Belly: I ne're more willing went (the Gods bee thanked)
Then now, when eah stepp leades to a goodly banquet.

Exit Belly & Cooke.

Sce: 3^{a}

Bread, Salt, Table. all stepp
forth againe and speake

Brea: How like you this M^{rs}, I still thought
The matter would at lenght to this bee brought.

Cush: That Belly can as well bee hang'd as keape
Himselfe from victualls, sure he eats in's sleape.
His meate into his gutts hee doth soe ramme in,
That sure hee'd dye should hee but heare of famine.

Salt: But to leave this, I thinke it best to goe
Into some inner roome. Tab: And I thinke soe
For if perhapps in fury they come by,

---

569 scollers] Another clear reference to the play's university origin.

574 eah] Apparently a misspelling for "each."

[V:1; V:2]

Faith Bread & Salt, & Trencher they must fly
Or whatsoe're come next. Therfore letts all
Stay i'th' next roome, still ready at their call.

Exeunt omnes.

Act 5 Sce: 1[a]

Enter at one dore King Beefe, Queene Mincepy,
S[r] Pepper, S[r] Vinigar, with Spitts & dripping
pannes, and such like weapons.

K: Bee: What not yet come King Brawne? then th'art a coward.
Speake good S[r] Vinigar, of our foes hast thou heard?
Vini: I heard but now (my Lord) they were a cōming.
K: Bee: It may bee true, for hearke I heare a drūming.

Sce: 2

Enter at the other dore King Brawne,
Lord Souce, S[r] Mustard W[th] weapons as beefore.

K: Bee: What? art thou come? I see thou keep'st thy word.
Braw: Yes Beefe & will maintaine it with my sword.
Descent from wordes to blowes upraiding varlet,
Thou art my object, with thy Queene that Harlot.
Q: Mince: What? doth hee call mee Harlot? stand aside.
By Cocke & Pie, Ile make the rogue one eyde.
K: Bee: But peace Faire Queene. But Brawne what do'st thou meane
To call our royall Queene as bad as Queane?
K: Braw: Ile make thee know that thou hast wrought flat treason
To depose us when thou art out of season.
Vini: Well Brawne for once I will say thou ly'st,

[V:3]

But if thou speake soe once againe thou dy'st.
Must: How now Sr Vinigar, are you soe lusty?
Ile pay you now, allthough my blade bee rusty.
Vini: Thou know'st not how to handle it I feare
Ile deale wth thee at cuffes. Mu: oh my ears { they pull one another by the eares

Sce: 3

Enter the Cooke with his Chopping
knife, with Belly.

Cooke: Shame take yee, that yee put mee to such feares
Who hath set you together by the eares?
K: Bee: I now here's one will fight with us I doubt mee
Cooke: Leave of you Vassailes, or I shall soe clout yee,
That I shall make yee all repent this trouble,
Which yee have put mee to treble & double.
Prostrate y^{r}selves, & lay y^{r} weapons downe Bell ꝑtes them
Doe yee not feare your lives, when wee but frowne?
Omnes: Wee doe, wee doe, wee doe.
Belly: Gods blessing on your heart, good Mr Cooke.
Hee provides meate, whil'st I but overlooke.
Cooke: Prostrate your selves yee whorsons at our feete,
Or else this chopping knife & your neckes shall meete.
K: Bee: King Beefe, who was your Viceroy, resignes now
His crowne and to your feete doth humbly bowe

[V:3]

K: Bra: And I but now a King. Sou: & I the Kings sonne
Give over to your mercy our Kingdome.
Q: Min: Good Mr Cooke for Gods sake pardon mee {She kneels downe
I am a silly woman as you see.
Cooke: Rise up, but I'le not brooke this bad uproare,
Beleive mee Sirs but yee have vext mee sore.
For wch thou Beefe in bonds of packthred tied,
Shall't first bee rosted, after broyl'd & fried.
And Mrs Mincepy 'cause you made such hast
To get forth, you shall bee inclosd in past,
With walls that shall surpasse these walls of mud,
Walls made of finest flower. Bel: oh this is good.
Cooke: As for Brawne, Mustard, Vinigar, Pepper, you
With Souce in your old mansions ay Ile mue.
Omnes: O spare good Mr Cooke this cruell labour.
Cooke: Cruell it is not, when you scorne our favour.
But if you'l yeald to bee serv'd in by mee,
Your punishmentes shall mitigated bee.
Omnes: Most willingly, most willingly. Coo: Then to tell yee
The trueth, your cheifest guest to night is Belly.
Omnes: Oh woefull! Coo: Belly goe thou in & stay,

---

638 Sou:] There seems to be no particular significance to the somewhat random underlining of some of these final speech headings, outside of distinguishing them from the speeches themselves. The practice does not occur earlier in the manuscript.

651 mue] Confine, shut up.

For preasently Ile send the meate away.
Belly: Make hast for Gods sake. Exit Belly.
Cooke: Brawne th'art first in order.
Souce stand you backe, Ile keepe you in my Larder.
Mustard, bee next thy M^{r} give attendance
For it you do'n't, Ile make you with a vengeance.
Beefe come thou next. Bee: I should have been the first.
Cooke: What doe yee prate? well you shall fare the worst.
Pepper & Vinigar, guard him well I pray,
For it is very like hee'l runne away.
You Mrs Mincepy shall alone bee sent.
Soe get yee in. Souce Ile keepe you till Lent
{ Exeunt omnes Manent Cooke & Souce }

Sce: 4^{a}

Cooke: The storme is past, this powerfull hand hath stilld
All troublous jarres: our Scene with peace is fill'd.
Noe scarre, nor breach our newborne quiet seavers:
If you'r pleas'd eyes, smile on our poor indevours.
With you I come to make yet one peace more,
Not with my chopping knife as heretofore;
But with this womans weapon to intreat,
Not to commande as earst I did the meate
For flowring stile, or phrase yee have it not,
I've learn'd noe more then how to boyle a pot.
This for our labour; if the subject fit not,

679 womans weapon] His tongue.

[V:4]

As beeing to grosse, 'tis hard though it hit not
The time right home noe matter how small reason
Y'ave rime, & though not good yet 'tis in season
If you are plead, loe heere a sutor standes
Wee neede noe Lawrell, crowne us wth your hands.
But if your eares bee griev'd with such a toy,
Y'are rid of us, and soe clapp hands for joy.

Finis.

---

687 sutor] In the sense of an "earnest seeker." He is, of course, seeking applause.

BIBLIOGRAPHY

Alton, R. E. , ed. "The Academic Drama in Oxford: Extracts from the Records of Four Oxford Colleges." Collections V. The Malone Society. Oxford: University Press, 1959, 29-95.

Anderson, John L., comp. A Fifteenth Century Cookry Boke. New York: Charles Scribner's Sons, 1962.

"Barton Holiday's Marriages of the Arts." The Retrospective Review, 8 (1823), 304-12.

Bentley, Gerald Eades. The Jacobean and Caroline Stage. 7 vols., 1941-56; rpt. Oxford: Clarendon, 1949-68.

Billington, Sandra. "Sixteenth-Century Drama in St. John's College, Cambridge." Review of English Studies, 29 (Frebrary 1978), 1-10.

Bland, D. S. "A Checklist of Drama at the Inns of Court." Research Opportunities in Renaissance Drama, 9 (1966), 47-61.

Boas, F. S. "Bibliography to Chapter XII: University Plays." In Cambridge History of English Literature, 6 (1961), 523-44.

________. "The Early Oxford Academic Stage." Oxford Magazine, XXX (1912), 240-42 and 259-60/

________. An Introduction to Stuart Drama. London: Oxford University Press, 1946.

________. "Recently Recovered Manuscripts at St. John's College, Oxford." Modern Language Review, 11 (1916), 298-301.

________. Shakespeare and the Universities. 1923; rpt. New York: Benjamin Blom, 1971.

________. "Theatrical Companies at Oxford in the Seventeenth Century." Fortnightly Review, 10 (1918), 256-62.

________. University Drama in the Tudor Age. 1914; rpt. New York: Benjamin Blom, 1966.

________. "University Plays." In The Cambridge History of English Literature, Vol. VI, The Drama to 1642: Part Two. Ed. A. W. Ward and A. R. Waller. Cambridge: Cambridge University Press, 1961, 293-327.

Bowers, Fredson. "Thomas Randolph's 'Salting.'" Modern Philology, 39 (1942), 275-80.

Bowers, R. H. "Some Folger Academic Drama Manuscripts." Studies in Bibliography, 12 (1959), 117-30.

Bradner, Leicester. "The Latin Drama of the Renaissance (1340-1640)." Studies in the Renaissance, 4 (1957), 31-54.

________. "The Rise of Secular Drama in the Renaissance." Studies in the Renaissance, 3 (1956), 7-22.

Brooke, C. F. Tucker. The Tudor Drama. Boston: Houghton Mifflin Co., 1911.

Byrne, Muriel St. Clare. Elizabethan Life in Town and Country. London: Methuen, 1961.

Charlton, Kenneth. Education in Renaissance England. Toronto: University of Toronto, 1965.

Cordeaux, E. H., and D. H. Merry. A Bibliography of Printed Words Relating to the University of Oxford. Oxford: Clarendon Press, 1968.

Costello, W. T. The Scholastic Curriculum at Early Seventeenth-Century Cambridge. Cambridge, Massachusetts: Harvard University Press, 1958.

Courtney, W. L. "Oxford Plays Down to the Restoration." Notes & Queries, 7th Series, 2 (1886), 464.

Dawson, Giles E. "An Early List of Elizabethan Plays." Library, 4th Series, 15 (1934-35), 445-56.

Dewey, Nicholas. "The Academic Drama of the Early Stuart Period (1603-1642): A Checklist of Secondary Sources." Research Opportunities in Renaissance Drama, 12 (1969). 33-42.

Dobson, E. J., ed. The Phonetic Writings of Robert Robinson. Early English Text Society, Ser. 1, No. 238. New York: Oxford University Press, 1957.

________. "Robert Robinson and His Phonetic Transcripts of Early Seventeenth-Century English Pronunciation." Transcactions of the Philological Society, 1947. London: David Tutt, 1948, pp. 25-63.

Duckworth, George E. The Nature of Roman Comedy. Princeton: Princeton University Press, 1971.

Eccles, Mark. "Francis Beaumont's Grammar Lecture." Review of English Studies, 16 (1940), 402-14.

Feldman, Sylvia D. The Morality-Patterned Comedy of the Renaissance. The Hague: Mouton, 1970.

Firth, Sir Charles. "Annals of the Oxford Stage." Oxford Magazine, 4 (1886), 65067.

Fleay, Frederick G. A Bibliographical Chronicle of the English Drama: 1559-1642, 2 Vols. New York; Burt Franklin, 1891.

________. A Chronicle History of the London Stage: 1559-1642. London: Reeves and Turner, 1890.

Green, A. Wigfall. The Inns of Court and Early English Drama. New York: Benjamin Blom, 1956.

Greg, W. W. Pastoral Poetry and Pastoral Drama. New York: Russell & Russell, 1959.

Guarna, Andreas. Bellum Grammaticale: A Discourse of Gret War and Dissention betweene Two Worthy Princes, the Noune and the Verbe. Tr. W[illiam] H[ayward]. London, 1576.

Hanford, James H. "The Debate Element in the Elizabethan Drama." Kittredge Anniversary Papers (1913), pp. 445-56.

________. "The Debate of Heart and Eye." Modern Language Notes, 26 (1911), 161-65.

Harbage, Alfred. Annals of English Drama: 975-1700. Rev. Samuel Schoenbaum. London: Methuen, 1964.

Harbage, Alfred. Cavalier Drama: An Historical and Critical Supplement to the Study of the Elizabethan and Restoration Stage. New York: Russell & Russell, 1964.

_______. "The Authorship of The Christmas Prince." Modern Language Notes, 50 (1935), 502.

_______. "Elizabethan and Seventeenth-Century Play Manuscripts." Publication of the Modern Language Association, 50 (1935), 687-99.

_______. "Elizabethan and Seventeen-Century Play Manuscripts: Addenda." Publication of the Modern Language Association, 52 (1937), 905-07.

Harrison, Molly. The Kitchen in History. Reading, U. K.: Osprey Publishing, 1972.

Harrison, William. Description of England. Ed. Georges Edelen. Ithaca, New York: Cornell University Press, 1968.

Henisch, Bridget Ann. Fast and Feast: Food in Medieval Society. University Park, Pennsylvania: The Pennsylvania State University Press, 1976.

Hosley, Richard. "The Formal Influence of Plautus and Terence." In Elizabethan Theatre, Stratford-upon-Avon Studies, 9, New York: St. Martin's Press, 1967 , 131-46.

[Hoadley, Samuel.] The Warr of Grammar (alternative title, Basileia seu Bellum Grammaticale). British Library Add. Ms. 22325.

Knights, L. C. "Education and the Drama in the Age of Shakespeare." Criterion, 11 (1932), 599-625.

[Knowles, W.?] "The Latin Plays Acted before the University of Cambridge." Retrospective Review, 12 (1825), 1-42.

Laidler, Josephine. "A History of Pastoral Drama in England until 1700." Englische Studien, 35 (1905), 193-259.

Latham, R. E. Revised Medieval-Latin Word-List from British and Irish Sources. London: Oxford University Press, 1965,

Leishman, J. B., ed. The Three Parnassus Plays (1598-1601). London: Ivor Nicholson and Watson, 1949.

Lily, William. A Shorte Introduction of Grammar. 1567; rpt. New York; Scholars' Facsimilies & Reprints, 1945,

MacKensie, W. Roy. The English Moralities from the Point of View of Allegory. Vol. 2 in Harvard Studies in English. New York: Gordian Press, 1966.

Mallett, Charles Edward. A History of the University of Oxford: Volume I, the Mediaeval University. New York: Longmans, Green and Co., 1924.

_______. A History of the University of Oxford: Volume II, the Sixteenth and Seventeenth Centuries. New York: Longmans, Green and Co., 1924.

Mead, William Edward. The English Mediaeval Feast. Boston: Houghton Mifflin, 1931.

Mills, L. J. "The Acting in University Comedy of Early Seventeenth-Century England." In Studies in the English Renaissance Drama in Memory of Karl J. Holzknecht. Eds. Josephine W. Bennett, Oscar Cargill, and Vernon Hall, Jr. New York: New York University Press, 1951, pp. 212-30.

Morgan, Louise B. "Some Academic Grammar Plays." Modern Language Review, 5 (1910), 199-200.

Motter, Thomas Hubbard Vail. The School Drama in England. New York: Longmans, Green and Co., 1929.

[Narcissus], a Twelfth Night Merriment. Ed. Margaret L. Lee. London: David Nutt, 1893.

Nichols, John G. The Progresses, Processions, and Magnificent Festivities of King James the First, His Royal Consort, Family and Court. 4 vols. London: J. B. Nichols, 1828.

Ong, Walter J. "Tudor Writings on Rhetoric." Studies in the Renaissance, 15 (1968), 39-69.

Pathomachia. Ed. Paul Edward Smith. Washington, D. C.: The Catholic University of America Press, 1942.

Prynne, William. Histriomastix, The Players Scourge, Or, Actors Tragedie. Ed. Arthur Freeman. New York: Garland Publishers, 1974.

Robertson, Roderick. "University Theatre at Oxford." Educational Theatre Journal, 8 (1956), 194-206.

Schelling, Felix E. Elizabethan Drama: 1558-1642. 2 vols. Boston and New York: Houghton Mifflin, 1908.

Smith, G. C. Moore, ed. "The Academic Drama at Cambridge: Extracts from College Records." Collections II, Part 2. The Malone Society. Oxford: University Press, 1923, pp. 150-231.

________. College Plays Performed in the University of Cambridge. Cambridge: Cambridge University Press, 1923.

________. "Notes on Some English University Plays." Modern Language Review, 3 (1908), 141-56.

Smith, Homer. "Pastoral Influence in the English Drama." Publication of the Modern Language Association, 12 (1897), 355-460.

Sonnino, Lee A. A Handbook to Sixteenth-Century Rhetoric. London: Rutledge and Kegan Paul, 1968.

Stratman, Carl J. "Dramatic Performances at Oxford and Cambridge, 1603-1642." Diss. University of Illinois, Urbana, 1947.

Stringer, Philip. "The Grand Reception and Entertainment of Queen Elizabeth at Oxford in 1592." Rpt. in Elizabethan Oxford: Reprints of Rare Tracts. Ed. Charles Plummer. Oxford: Clarendon Press, 1887.

Tanselle, G. Thomas. "Some Principles for Editorial Apparatus." Studies in Bibliography (1972), 41-88.

Taylor, E. S., and others. The History of Playing Cards. Rutland, Vermont: Charles E. Tuttle Company, 1973.

Tomkis, Thomas. Lingua. In Robert Dodsley. A Select Collection of Old English Plays. 4th ed. W. Carew Hazlitt, ed. 1874-76; rpt. New York: Benjamin Blom, 1964.

Tucker Brooke, C. F. "Latin Drama in Renaissance England." Journal of English Literary History, 13 (December 1946), 233-40.

Ward, Adolphus W. A History of English Dramatic Literature to the Death of Queen Anne. 3 vols. London: Macmillan & Company, 1899. Vol. II: "The Academical Drama," pp. 630-42. Vol. III: "Academical Plays," pp. 174-88.

Wilson, Frank Percy. The English Drama: 1485-1585. Ed. with Bibliography by G. K. Hunter. Vol. IV, Part 1 of The Oxford History of English Literature. Ed. Bonamy Dobree and Norman Davis. New York: Oxford University Press, 1969.

Wickham, Glynne. Early English Stages: 1300-1660. Volume Two, 1576 to 1660, Part II. New York: Columbia University Press, 1972.

Withington, Robert. English Pageantry: An Historical Outline. Cambridge, Massachusetts: Harvard University Press, 1918-20.

Wood, Anthony à. Athenae Oxonienses. Ed. Philip Bliss. 5 vols. London: F. C. & J. Rivington, 1813-20.

For Product Safety Concerns and Information please contact our EU representative GPSR@taylorandfrancis.com
Taylor & Francis Verlag GmbH, Kaufingerstraße 24, 80331 München, Germany

www.ingramcontent.com/pod-product-compliance
Lightning Source LLC
Chambersburg PA
CBHW051644230426
43669CB00013B/2432

* 9 7 8 1 1 3 8 2 3 9 9 5 1 *